Fieldbook
of
Nature
Photography

A Sierra Club Totebook®

Fieldbook of Nature Photography

By Patricia Maye

with a foreword
by Ansel Adams
and drawings
by Nicholas Fasciano

Sierra Club Books • San Francisco

The Sierra Club, founded in 1892 by John Muir, has devoted itself to the study and protection of the nation's scenic and ecological resources — mountains, wetlands, woodlands, wild shores and rivers. All club publications are part of the nonprofit effort the club carries on as a public trust. There are some 50 chapters coast to coast, and in Hawaii, Alaska and Canada. Participation is invited in the club's program to enjoy and preserve wilderness everywhere. Address: 530 Bush Street, San Francisco, California 94108.

Foreword

Wilderness experience is intimate and mystical. For many it becomes a dominant factor in their lives, creating a vast store of memories which protect them from the dross experiences of the world about them. The fact that wilderness experience *is* mystical — quite contrary to ideas of wilderness as a hostile environment — renders it all the more personal and precious. A few generations ago wilderness was something to be encountered and overcome. Demons inhabited the mountain fastnesses; starvation and death were the tolls exacted by the deserts, the barren lands, the rigors of winter and the threat of savage resistance. Now, equipped with the amenities of civilization, we enter wilderness protected from all hazards as were the first astronauts walking on the moon. There is scarcely a wild area that we cannot penetrate with almost total security. Our experiences become life-long engravings on the mind and spirit.

Since the advent of the camera we have not only augmented and perpetuated our experiences, but we have made it possible to communicate them to others, in greater or lesser degree as we are capable of using photography in both imaginative and technical ways. Undoubtedly, there is some ego involved — "See where I was and what I did, etc." There is also some of the collector's mania for maintaining a visual diary. Most important and rewarding, however, is the opportunity for the photographer to transmit experience, and I believe every person who cares in any way for the natural scene wishes to share the moments of beauty and wonder that have been his good fortune to encounter.

People of the out-of-doors flock together in a strong bond of purpose and dedication. Their community is not as large as it should be or as they think it is. The hard fact remains that the majority of human beings have little or no contact with nature except on the most bitter, frugal terms. Wilderness is to be shunned, or exploited materialistically, or used as a shallow "get-away-from-it-all" escape. Yet through education, visual and otherwise, the potential of wild places as a spiritual resource are slowly but surely being recognized.

Of course, man remains of supreme importance and the problem is to adjust the nature of man to the nature of the world, so that man may comprehend and use the world without destroying it or himself. The battle for this balance has just been joined, but emotional concepts are not enough. Philosophic and social realities must also be recognized. Education and communication are our strongest weapons. Here, photography may achieve impressive results.

The average photographer makes records of scenes, events, people and wildlife; anything and everything seen can be photographed (and much more besides). He captures the "external event" — the world of "reality," the world of space and time surrounding him. His pictures, even if poor as imagery, can recreate situations and events that have real present and future meaning. Any photograph, no matter how "realistic," is nothing but a recollection. The more accurate the image, the more information it conveys. But if this were all there was to photography, the automatic camera and the casual eye would combine to produce only a rather sterile diary of day-by-day experience.

The "internal event" implies another realm of experience. The realities of the external event pass through the eye-mind-spirit of the photographer and are transformed into interpretation and expression. The shapes of the external world are perceived as forms, augmented by management of the camera-optical image, exposure and development of the negative and the controls of photographic printing. Another order of vision appears; aesthetic qualities enlarge the emotional potentials of the literal image.

As Alfred Stieglitz so clearly stated, art in photography is the production of the Equivalent. By this he implied that something in the world is recognized or perceived, emotionally and aesthetically reacted to, and so recorded. The image is presented to the spectator; he may reject it as meaningless to him, he may respond to what the photographer intended, or he may receive a new world of vision and excitement from it. The creative photograph relates to much more than factual representation; some departure from reality is essential.

The important photographs of the natural scene are not realistic in the general sense, and the usual books and magazines of travel and nature weave a spectacular web of the obvious to entrap us. Colors are garish; compositions, obvious or strained; the mood, one of "enjoyment" (a poor substitute for "participation").

What is deeply felt cannot be verbalized (unless we are poets), so we must recognize the internal event as an intuitive condition. In the presence of a subject of potential interest and appeal we should visualize the optimum image of the print or transparency before the act of exposure. Practiced technique and experience lead to efficient intuitive accomplishment. What we see "out there" is chaos; what we see within is form and expression. All technical procedures, including the zone system, are valid only if they permit us to achieve fluent creative expression.

Virtuosity often inhibits creativity. People fear the supreme performer; his technique, repertory and public image. They become timid in the presence of great ability. This is unfortunate, for virtuosity does not necessarily relate to creative capacity or accomplishment. Everyone with a dream or a desire can create objects or images of beauty. Quite often someone unknown produces a remarkable work of art — perhaps a masterpiece or, at least, a *communication* of true importance.

When one enters the wilderness with his camera, assuming he does so with a spirit of mystical participation, he should trust his reactions and his visions. If he is capable he can create images that tell about the subject in both factual and emotional ways, and he can also tell about himself and his creative vision. He can create new vistas of imagination and excitement and add new dimensions to the experience of the natural scene.

This book contains a wealth of valuable information which should clarify many of the inevitable problems of the photographer in the out-of-doors. Much of the book should be studied at home and in the laboratory. The essential problems of field-work will be clarified through practice. "Dry-shooting" — practicing camera set-ups, organizations and compositions, scanning subjects with the Wratten #90 viewing filter for value-relationships in black and white work, experimenting with filters and polarizers and exposure-development determinations — represents a most valuable means of acquiring technique and general facility. Working out basic problems while striving for purely expressive results may reduce the effectiveness of both. "When you play when you practice, you will practice when you play" is an old musical adage applicable to photography.

Above all, the aspiring photographer should be constantly *observing* and *visualizing as images* the myriad aspects of the world around him. He must think of his eye as the camera eye and his vision as related to the response of the sensitive emulsions. He must learn to anticipate form, line, color, depth, texture, value and "presence," and how to control them by appropriate applications of the techniques of the great modern art-form of photography.

Ansel Adams
Carmel, Calif.
May, 1974

Contents

Illustrations and Tables

Introduction

Nature photography requires but two things: a reasonable level of photographic skill and a lively sensitivity to the natural world. Assuming that you are already possessed of an interest in nature — why else would you be inspired to photograph it? — the necessary photographic equipment and skills can be acquired with little money and lots of practice. Nature photography is not some secret specialty requiring gimmicks and arcane tricks. Chances are you can do a lot with the camera and accessories you already own if your eyes and your heart are in the right place.

The photographic possibilities in nature are so many and so varied that you may be challenged to reach beyond your present level of expertise, to follow some new direction. For the practiced amateur as well as the beginner, this is likely to involve equipment and techniques not in the standard repertoire. This book covers the basics as well as more advanced photographic lore, to provide an introduction to nature photography.

Eight Photographs

Photos and commentaries by

Ansel Adams
Ed Cooper
Dennis Stock
Richard Kauffman
Patricia Caulfield
Les Line
Philip Hyde
Douglas Faulkner

A meaningful photograph begins with some recognition of the qualities of the subject to which we have a personal response. It is usually a rather "immediate" happening; seldom the result of prolonged thought. The artist frequently responds to some creative symbolism in his subject — yet this may be an unconscious awareness on his part which is transmitted to the spectator in a variety of interpretations. To attempt "verbal explanation" of the image or to impose fixed interpretations will simply ruin the experience for the spectator.

My response to this subject was truly immediate. It was suddenly there before me and was quickly visualized as an image. Fortunately, my technique was adequate to compose and expose in reference to the image desired. Unfortunately, I had only a rather long-focus lens and could not get the full depth of field I wanted. I could stop the lens down only to $f/16$; the exposure had to be short enough to arrest movement of the grass blades in the slight wind.

People have asked me "what does this picture mean?" I reply that I do not know what it *means* — only that it *feels* to me very much what I felt when first confronted with the subject. The artist must not impose reactions or interpretations on his audience; his obligation is to select and interpret beauty, to create "equivalents" (Alfred Stieglitz's term) of what he felt, and to present his images — without restrictions of meaning — to the world at large.

Ansel Adams
Carmel, California

If desert plants and flowers appeal to you as a photographer, then the place to be is Baja California. In many places there, yucca and cactus may be found only a few yards above the high-tide line. Perhaps nowhere else in the world does the desert meet the ocean in such a spectacular array of forms and colors.

This particular yucca was one of a group of thousands in a large cluster, about a mile from the ocean. I have always been fascinated by the patterns to be found in nature, and as I gazed over the field of yuccas, my eye was immediately drawn to this one. I was fascinated by the pattern of the tips repeating themselves; by the color contrast of the red and the green. So I zeroed in on this pattern and made it full frame for maximum visual effect. With a high overcast, the lighting was ideal. I used a view camera, 4 x 5, to help me capture the intimate detail of the plant. I took a number of exposures, bracketing them. The film used was Ektachrome.

Ed Cooper
Seattle, Washington

Much of what I prefer to photograph in nature is that which most people step on. Blades of grass, weeds, and alienated twigs readily inspire me. The minutiae discovered in the estuary, desert, or meadow often contain as much visual drama as a classic vista of a canyon, mountain, or coastline. The task is to set one's sights for the subtleties rather than the obvious. To be attuned to detail doesn't preclude landscape coverage. It simply alerts the mind to the multiplicity of photographic potential when entering nature's arena.

My images are viewed through a 35 mm single-lens reflex camera — ideally suited for full-frame composition and "get-what-you-see" exactitude.

To articulate an appreciation of nature's graphics, I principally work with shallow-depth optics and selective focusing. Composition and depth control are the main forces in guiding the camera to a satisfactory frame. The shutter speed chosen should support the initial perception.

A testy atmosphere of changing light and capricious winds increases my concentration. I reach for an essence. And sometimes succeed.

Dennis Stock
Woodstock, New York

This picture, from a book of my photographs called *Gentle Wilderness: The Sierra Nevada*, is one of my favorites. I feel that it contrasts the frail and evanescent quality of the flower with the massive timelessness of the Devils Postpile.

This crystalline basalt formation by itself would afford many an interesting study for the black-and-white photographer, but because of the unrelieved gray of the rock, a touch of color must be introduced for an effective color picture. After exploring around the base for a while, I found what I wanted, set up my camera on the tripod, waited until the sun back-lit the flower to my satisfaction, and then released the shutter.

Here is some photographic data: All my pictures are taken on 2¼ x 3¼ film. This is the maximum size available on roll film. I prefer the 4 x 5 format, but a 2¼ x 3¼ camera, tripod, three or four lenses, and film weigh over 25 pounds, and when backpacking, this is sufficient. Essential to me when doing nature photography is a camera with front and back swings to obtain maximum depth of field. This picture represents the use of back swings on a Linhof Technica camera.

Richard Kauffman
San Francisco, California

Felis concolor — panther, puma, cougar, mountain lion, call it what you will — is an endangered species. This particular animal was photographed (for the book *Everglades*) after its release in Everglades National Park. An effort was underway at the time to repopulate the park with great cats, and I was fortunate to be on hand when this individual was given its freedom in the saw grass. The cat showed no hostility or fear. It simply stalked off a hundred feet or so and sat down in the grass. It was hot — thus, the open, panting jaws. I remember as I prepared to frame the cat that a jet crossed the sky above us. The cat looked up. I used a 300 mm *f*/4.5 Auto-Nikkor lens.

Patricia Caulfield
New York, New York

When I photograph wildflowers, or other small growing things like ferns or fungi or seedlings, I am looking for more than a documentary picture of a blossom or a plant. I want to capture, on film, the *essence* of a living species – where it grows, how it grows. I want to show the flower as it might be discovered by an inquisitive person exploring a woodland or a meadow.

The portrait of bloodroot is an example. I have seen many pictures staring straight down at those showy white petals. They say nothing. But this photograph tells a story. It says that the bloodroot is one of the very first wildflowers of spring, appearing through the drab leaf mold in March and April when the deciduous forest is a monochromatic brown. It shows how the bloodroot's stems are embraced by deeply lobed leaves.

Selective focus sharply isolates the bloodroot from the background, but there is still a suggestion, a *feeling*, of leafless trees marching up a hill. Large format photographers, of course, abhor any out-of-focus areas in their pictures. I put them to use, choosing an aperture so that the primary subject is defined while its habitat is *perceived.*

My wildflower portraits all are taken in natural light, with a hand-held camera. I use a Nikon F single-lens reflex; for woodland flowers, the lens is almost exclusively a 55mm Micro-Nikkor. For meadow flowers, I often use a 280mm Novaflex with bellows.   *Les Line*
                              New York, New York

There has been a tendency among "color" photographers to emphasize the bizarre in color. It is a tendency that conservative publishers and slick magazines have overplayed ever since color materials first became available in photography. But for me, the color photograph, to express some kind of lasting meaning, needs subtlety and staying power. It needs content.

The Sierra Nevada, as most mountain ranges, is a difficult color subject precisely because its color palette is subtle, and its brightest colors are found principally in its smallest objects, as in flowers, or an occasional dead tree trunk (Kings Canyon detail, opposite.) Its mass is granite, a nominal gray (that can be made gorgeous in certain light). Browns and greens predominate where the granite has been tamed by the elements. Nice colors to live with, but no show-stoppers.

As to equipment, the kind of camera or lens is not so important as one's ability to use it — and to be fluid with it under field conditions. Which translates into experience, and the only way you get that is by going out and *doing*. The world is full of "photographers" whose chief activity seems to be fondling or discussing their cameras. And that's too bad, because cameras don't make pictures. People do.

Philip Hyde
Taylorsville, California

Photography is the hunting instinct carried over. Much of the secret of a good nature photograph is in understanding the animal so as not to alarm it. The rest of the secret is in the heart. As much as possible I have become a non-trespasser, but if the subject is aware of my presence I try to record the fish's reaction of curiosity or wonder in my presence. I do not always succeed, but as often as possible my ideal is to show our encounter, or at least what I find beautiful. At such moments, I am one with the alien being who is no less a wondrous personage than an inhabitant of another planet. As with this longspine squirrel fish from Caribbean waters, our eyes have met. Knowing now the vulnerability of the sea and her children, I would hope that my personal view may awaken in humans a sense of kinship with other expressions of life. A diving friend, Yves Merlet, once said of a giant sea bass that had alarmed me, "Why, they are friendly people."

Douglas Faulkner
Summit, New Jersey

Notes on the Photographers

Ansel Adams: The distinguished dean of American nature photography, tutor to three generations of photographers. . . .works include *This Is the American Earth*, *My Camera in the National Parks*, *Illustrated Guide to Yosemite Valley*, *The Basic Photo Series*, and many others.

Ed Cooper: A refugee of Wall Street, now a free-lancer residing in the Northwest. . . .works almost exclusively with the 4 x 5 view camera. . . . contributor to *Alpine Lakes* and *The Wild Places*. . . .his photographs have also appeared in *Audubon* and *Backpacker*.

Dennis Stock: Member of Magnum Photos. . . . author of a number of photographic books and portfolios, including *Brother Sun*, *Circle of Seasons*, *National Parks Centennial Portfolio*, *Jazz Street*, *California Trip* and *The Alternative*. . . . work has appeared in *Life*, *Look*, *Holiday*, *Venture*.

Richard Kauffman: President of a San Francisco printing firm and expert color lithographer. . . . one-man shows at Eastman House, Los Angeles

County Museum and San Francisco Museum of
Art....published works include *Gentle Wilderness: The Sierra Nevada* in the Sierra Club
Exhibit Format Series.

Patricia Caulfield: Former executive editor of *Modern Photography*....resigned in 1967 to devote
her career to nature photography....her photographs have appeared in *Audubon* and *Natural
History* magazines and she is the author of *Everglades* in the Sierra Club Exhibit Format Series.

Les Line: Editor of *Audubon* Magazine, the nation's most beautifully illustrated environmental
journal....his photographs illustrate a number of
juvenile books and he is co-author as well of
Seasons and *The Sea Has Wings*.

Philip Hyde: Interpreter of the American wilderness....his major photographic works include *Island in Time*, *The Last Redwoods*, *Navajo Wildlands*, *Slickrock*, and *Mountain and Desert*, all
published under the imprint of Sierra Club Books.

Douglas Faulkner: One of the world's foremost
underwater photographers....student of marine
biology....his pictures have been on display at the
American Museum of Natural History....co-author
of *The Hidden Sea*.

Your Equipment

You can photograph nature subjects with whatever equipment you already own. The working suggestions in the later chapters of this book will apply no matter what your equipment may be. This chapter, however, will discuss the various types of cameras and accessories available, to help you better understand their special applications to nature photography, better comprehend the assets and shortcomings of whatever camera you may already own, or help you decide what equipment and accessories you might like to buy to establish or expand your basic photographic outfit.

Cameras

A camera can be described in terms of two basic characteristics: its format — the size of the film it uses and the negatives it produces — and its viewing system. The phrase "35mm camera" seems descriptive enough; but it tells us only what size film a camera uses. It is at least as important to know what kind of viewing system a camera has, for this is the feature that most affects the way a camera works. The four main types of viewing systems are the single-lens reflex, rangefinder, twin-lens reflex, and view; each has its strong points and shortcomings for nature photography.

The Single-Lens Reflex Camera

The single-lens reflex camera is the most varied and popular type on the market today. Familiarly known as the SLR, it offers the greatest adaptability to the widest range of subjects, and it is especially useful for coping with the infinite diversity of nature.

SLR viewing: When you view your subject with an SLR, you are seeing as your lens "sees." The accompanying diagram illustrates the circuitous course of the image: through the lens via a mirror to a ground glass and then reversed by a prism before reaching your eye. This indirect and complicated viewing system permits you to view the image exactly as it will appear on your film. Precise framing, subject size, depth of field, exact focus, can all be checked and adjusted before you take your picture. Most pictorial effects you may wish to include – from filter to soft-focus – can be previewed. If both camera and photographer are in working order, then what you see is what you get.

SLR formats: Most SLRs – Nikons, Pentaxes, Minoltas, and others – use 35mm films, widely available in neat, compact, light-tight cassettes containing either 20 or 36 frames. Each frame measures 24mm x 36mm, about 1'' x 1½''. Large SLRs – Hasselblads and Bronicas, for instance –

Single-Lens Reflex Cameras

Single-Lens Reflex Viewing

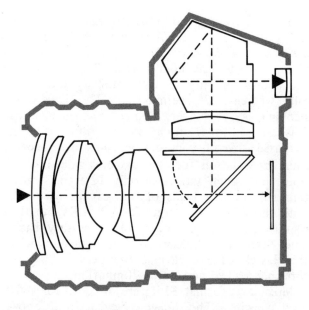

The single-lens reflex is the most popular type of camera today. Such compact, well designed models as the 35mm Nikkormat (left top) prove to be versatile enough to fill almost any imaginable nature photography need. The larger Hasselblad offers many of the features of the 35mm SLR plus a larger film size but fewer exposures per standard roll of film. With the prism-equipped SLR, viewing is done directly through the lens and the image appears in the viewer just as it will appear on the film. As shown in the diagram above, the image enters the lens, is reflected off a mirror set at a 45-degree angle within the camera, passes through the prism mounted on top of the camera, and finally reaches the eye right-side-up and laterally correct. Most large format SLR s do not come with the prism as original equipment. The image appears for viewing on a ground glass on the camera top. It is right-side-up but laterally reversed.

offer the advantage of a larger frame size. They use 120 or 220 roll films and yield frames of either 2½" x 2¼" or 2¼" x 2¾". The two roll films, 120 and 220, both measure 2¼" across, but 120 allows for only 12 shots of 2¼" x 2¼" per roll, whereas 220 permits 20. The larger film size allows for bigger, clearer enlargements than those possible from a 35mm film. But the increased size of your enlargements may seem a small consolation for the loss of a once-in-a-life-time shot when you have only 12 frames rather than 36. Longer loads of film can be used with both the 35mm and larger format SLRs, but they require the purchase of special accessory backs. One Nikon back allows for 250 exposures while the Hasselblad No. 70 magazine permits 70 exposures per load of perforated 70mm film.

Most large-format SLRs are designed for waist-level viewing. The image, viewed from above, appears on the ground glass right side up but reversed from left to right. The Honeywell Pentax 6 x 7 is one exception — looking and operating like an enlarged prism-equipped 35mm SLR. Framing, especially tracking subjects in reversed motion on a ground glass, is a tricky business that has been eliminated by the prism in 35mm SLRs. Prism viewers for eye-level, laterally correct viewing are available as an expensive accessory for some 2¼" x 2¼" SLRs.

SLR Standard Formats

Contact prints from standard frames of 35mm and 120 (2¼" x 2¼") films are reproduced actual size above. The larger size of the 120 frame allows for finer detail in large-scale reproduction or enlargement.

The larger the film format, the larger the camera. Thus, the 120 SLRs are heavier and more cumbersome than their 35mm cousins — a vital consideration in the field. Films are more expensive per frame and less widely available. And if your final aim is to produce color slides for projection, you'll need a projector specially designed to accept 120 slides. On the other hand, the larger format cameras do produce spectacular images, legible and practical. Their extra bulk, weight, and clumsiness can be forgiven in static situations such as landscape photography. Indeed, many professionals rely on them exclusively for such shots, especially because publishers prefer the larger transparencies for color reproduction.

Operation of the SLR: Once you've set your camera for the prevailing light conditions and focused on the subject, it is simply a matter of pushing the button. Inside the camera, photography is a great deal more complicated than that. (As illustrated, the internal operation of an SLR is especially complicated.) As you push the shutter release, the viewing mirror that deflects the image to your eye must swing up to allow the image to pass through to the film. Only then is the shutter released. That's with the simplest SLR. Add to this sequence the operation of the array of automatic features with which SLRs now are equipped, and you become aware that the modern SLR is a highly complex, delicate machine. Its detractors like to insist that the SLR is always waiting for the most inopportune moment to break down. Not so, with care — but the SLR does require care.

Available accessories and features of the SLR: SLR manufacturers seem to be involved in an endless gimmickry sweepstakes. Each year with great fanfare new models are introduced, loaded with an increasing number of novelties and accessories (at increased cost, needless to say). For the sake of simplicity and economy, only the features most useful in nature photography with the SLR are included here. Some of the more fanciful innovations will be mentioned, or ignored, in later sections.

So diverse are the subjects you'll encounter in nature that the ability to switch lenses should be the first prerequisite in your choice of camera. Lens interchangeability, along with through-the-lens viewing (which permits you to witness the effect of your lens choice), are the strongest selling points for the SLR.

When the mirror in your SLR viewing system flips up to allow the image to hit the film, the viewer goes dark. Most recent models return the mirror to viewing position as soon as the exposure is made, thereby restoring your image view. As

Typical SLR Exposure Sequence

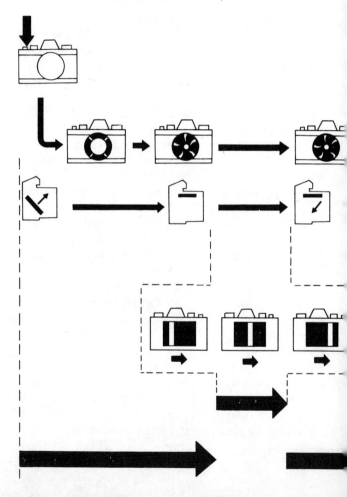

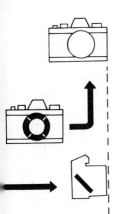

When you press the shutter release on most modern SLRs equipped with an automatic lens and focal-plane shutter, the story's just begun. As shown in the diagram at left, first the lens is shut down to a preset opening and the viewing mirror within the camera flips up to allow the light to pass through to the film. Then the shutter passes across the film at a preset speed. Finally the lens opens up again to maximum aperture and the mirror is returned to viewing position.

quickly as this happens — and it is quick — the mirror action must be considered. You must also learn to accept a momentary blackout of your vision while the picture is actually being taken. Although brief, this blind moment can prove bothersome in photographing fast-moving animals or birds. You must anticipate your exposure by a fraction of a second, "leading" a moving subject just as a rifleman leads the prey in his gunsights, in order to give the mirror time to get out of the way and let the film record the exact moment you want.

In non-automatic models the situation is much worse for the nature photographer because the mirror must be returned to viewing position manually with the advance of the film. Even the most dexterous and quick-witted photographers find this a great obstacle to rapid-sequence, accurate shooting. Happily, most manufacturers have eliminated the problem, but check before buying.

The light meter is probably the most frequently used accessory. SLRs allow for metering directly through the lens, eliminating the need for any intermediate *and* time-consuming calculations. But many built-in meters are the averaging type, which make no special note of the problems you will encounter or the special effects you may want to achieve. Many professionals scorn built-ins, citing as shortcomings their inexactness, additional on-camera weight, the distraction of needles and marks in the viewer as they are trying to frame, and the frequency of malfunctions. (Meters are discussed in greater detail later in this chapter.)

Most SLRs offer a system of interchangeable parts. To the camera body — merely a light-tight box with a built-in shutter — you can add viewers, focusing screens, filters, motor-driven film advances, lighting units, and other special apparatus, as well as lenses of almost any focal length, to adapt your camera to an infinite variety of situations and purposes. Adaptability should be a strong consideration in the purchase of a camera — and adaptability is best spelled "SLR." With an eye to the future, find out what useful accessories are available for the camera you're choosing, and you'll end up with a flexible system of equipment. You can expand your basic equipment to deal with nature subjects ranging from photomicroscopy of the tiniest creatures to telephotography of the distant planets.

The Rangefinder Camera

The 35mm rangefinder camera, like the 35mm SLR, is light, compact, and takes the handy 35mm film cassettes. Unlike the SLR, the rangefinder camera has a viewing system that is independent of the camera's optics. The image is seen through a small window at the top or side of the camera. The view-finder image allows for framing and cropping, while a small portion in the center is used for focusing. Exact focus is achieved by bringing a split or double image in the center of the view into alignment. When the camera is out of focus, the image remains split or broken; when it is in focus, the images merge. Although viewing and focusing are not done through the lens as with the SLR, the focusing device on most contemporary rangefinder cameras is coupled to the lens − as the split image in the viewer is aligned the coupled lens is extended or retracted to the correct focusing distance.

The viewing system of the rangefinder camera works well for large-scale subjects at reasonable distances. Indeed, rangefinder fans emphasize the fact that with this viewing system − especially with wide-angle lenses, which are difficult to focus exactly with the SLR − the subject is clearly either in or out of focus, and focusing is quick and exact, even in dim light.

However, as the viewing is not done through the lens, any magnification of the subject offered by the use of long, or telephoto, lenses is not apparent in the viewer. Framing is done by centering the subject within sets of etched lines that indicate the cropping. The number of lines that can be included in one viewfinder is limited, and this limits the choice of lenses that can be used without accessory

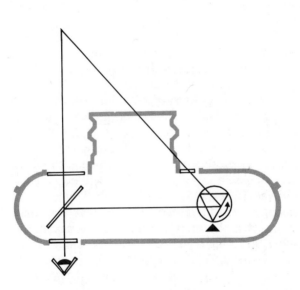

With the rangefinder, the viewing image does not enter through the lens. It enters instead through a small window above and to the side of the lens. A second image enters through another window at the opposite side. A prism behind the second window rotates to bring the images into alignment. As the prism rotates the coupled lens moves forward or back. When the image appears clear in the viewer, the lens is focused.

viewfinders. Long telephotos, essential to photographing distant wildlife, cannot be accurately focused with a basic rangefinder. So the rangefinder camera has trouble with long shots.

There are also some problems with close-ups. The rangefinder camera's separate viewing system "sees" from a slightly different point of view than the taking lens. You can demonstrate the effect of the twin points of view with your own eyes. Cover one eye and look at an object in the distance. Then cover the viewing eye and look at the object with the other eye. Then, repeat the exercise with an object at close range — a raised finger held about ten inches in front of your face will do nicely. You will notice two things — that the object seems to change position as you switch eyes and that the closer it is the more it seems to move. And, at the close shooting range you may be using in nature work, this difference in viewpoint becomes critical. It can mislead you into framing and focusing on a lovely bud, but ending up with a shot of its stem. This shift in view is called parallax.

The separate view also makes it difficult to compose in depth. You may want the limb of a foreground tree to come only so far into the picture. Unless you take into account the position of the viewer in relation to your lens, you may well find that your careful composition comes to naught. Finally, the separate viewer of the rangefinder permits viewing, focusing, and picture taking with the lens cap in place or a stray finger or neck strap in front of the lens — unlikely sounding propositions until you have succeeded at any or all of them, and you will.

Some rangefinder cameras, including the Leica, offer a reflex housing as an accessory. Inserted between the lens and camera body, it essentially converts the rangefinder camera into an SLR to allow for close-up and long-distance photography.

In its favor, the rangefinder camera is lighter and less complicated than the SLR. Because of its comparative mechanical simplicity it is less prone to malfunctions and costly repair. Interchangeable lenses are available for the more expensive models, and if you exceed a limited range of focal lengths, you can purchase supplementary viewfinders.

The Twin-Lens Reflex Camera

Twin-lens reflex cameras — Rolleiflex, Mamiya, for example — have, as the name implies, two lenses. "Reflex" suggests that the viewing optics resemble those of the SLR. Indeed they do — to a point. The image enters the top lens, strikes a mirror angled at 45 degrees, and is projected onto a ground glass for viewing and focusing from above. The top lens is used for viewing only. The picture is taken through the bottom lens, which projects more or less the same image onto the film. The two

Twin-Lens Reflex Camera

Like the rangefinder, the twin-lens reflex camera has separate
viewing and picture-taking systems. Like the SLR, the TLR has a
mirror inside to reflect the image for viewing. As the diagram shows,
the image enters the TLR through two lenses. The image from the
top lens is reflected off a 45-degree mirror for viewing from above as
it appears on a ground glass. Like all mirror images, this viewing

Twin-Lens Reflex Viewing

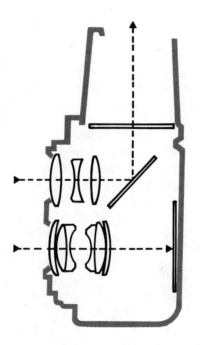

image is reversed from left to right. The image entering through the lower lens goes straight through to the film when the shutter is released.

The Mamiya C330 shown at left differs from most TLRs in that it offers a selection of interchangeable lenses.

lenses are coupled, so as you focus the image through the viewing lens, the taking lens follows dutifully along. The image on the ground glass is large (2¼" x 2¼"). Magnifiers, often built into the viewing system, make critical focusing possible. But, for lack of a prism, the image appears on the viewing screen laterally reversed. And, because of the separation between the viewing and taking lenses, the shot framed on the ground glass will be a little different from the image on the film, just as with the rangefinder camera. (A solution to this parallax problem will be found in the chapter on *Close-ups.*) The TLR uses 120 or 220 roll film. Few models allow for interchangeable lenses; the Mamiya C is one popular exception. The TLR's simplicity of design and operation, large format, sturdiness, and relatively reasonable price have maintained its popularity despite its limitations.

The View Camera

The continued, if limited, popularity of the cumbersome view camera testifies to the unwillingness of dedicated photographers to abandon a good and useful tool. This odd, seemingly complicated device is actually the oldest and most rudimentary of all adjustable cameras.

At one time the view camera was *it* — there was simply nothing else that the photographers could use. And use it they did — men like William Henry

Jackson, who photographed America's grand Western wilderness and then familiarized all of America with the region's beauty through publication and distribution of his splendid photographs; or the Bisson brothers, whose expedition reached and photographed the highest peaks of the Alps. Despite its bulk and technical limitations, in the hands of such men, the view camera was capable of making photographs that are still admired as art. Although lighter, quicker, more economical cameras have been introduced in the interim, many serious professionals still rely on the view camera as their primary tool for landscape work. The exquisite detail and richness to be found in the view-camera work of such modern masters as Ansel Adams and Eliot Porter, and a constant crop of younger photographers, demonstrate the undying value of the view camera.

A view camera is made up simply of a lens-and-shutter assembly at the front and a ground-glass viewing screen at the back, connected by a light-tight, accordion-pleated bellows. The image enters the lens and appears upside-down and backward on the ground glass. Focusing is done by moving or "racking" the lens panel back and forth on a track until the image is sharp. The familiar black cloth under which photographers have been hiding for over a century is necessary to keep stray light off the surface of the ground glass, making

The view camera is the largest and simplest of the cameras discussed in this section. Seen from the front, the Sinar model shown seems relatively unimpressive. The profile is more interesting and more telling of the flexibility of this large-format camera.

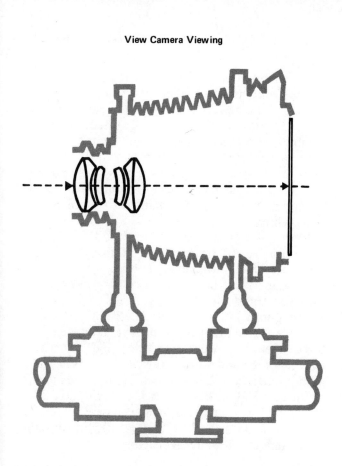

Viewing with the view camera is direct. The image passed through the lens, travels down the light-tight bellows, and appears on the ground glass at the rear of the camera, as shown in the diagram. Because of the action of the lens, the image on the ground glass is upside down and reversed. For picture taking, a sheet of film is inserted just in front of the ground glass.

the image brighter and easier to focus.

The front and rear elements of the ideal view camera — the lens and film plane — can be raised, lowered, moved sideways, and tilted, with the flexible bellows keeping the unit light-tight. The view camera's unique contortions allow the photographer to perform visual stunts with the subject before him. The techniques of control are called "image management" for want of a more artistic term, which they truly deserve.

View cameras come in 3¼" x 4¼", 4" x 5", 5" x 7", and 8" x 10" sizes. Film is relatively expensive and not widely available. The cameras are unwieldly and must be mounted on a tripod when in use. The upside-down and reversed image makes action photography impossible. But view camera champions claim that the expense and unwieldiness force them to work carefully and selectively instead of banging away like Machine Gun Kelly with a cartridge-loaded 35mm. And the exquisite detail in a 3¼" x 4¼", 4" x 5", 5" x 7", or 8" x 10" negative or transparency, compared with the detail in a 35mm, 1" x 1½" frame, remains the view camera's unchallenged strong point.

Lenses

Generally, nature photography's subject is anything under the sun that got there without man's help. By the same token, the nature photographer is the most versatile of all photographers. In a single day in the field you may feel moved to photograph a vast and open landscape, a bird soaring overhead, a tiny wildflower or mushroom. But to be *that* versatile, you need a versatile camera, one that can accept a variety of lenses of different focal lengths.

The manufacturer may offer a dozen lenses of different focal lengths for use with your camera body. In a complete 35mm SLR system — Nikon, for instance — the available focal lengths range all the way from 6mm through 2000mm. Your arsenal of lenses should be a personal choice, based on the type of work you intend to do. The major factors in your selection should be: 1) the focal length of the lens; 2) the lens' "speed," or maximum amount of light admitted by the lens; and 3) automatic features.

Lenses to Fit Your Camera

Naturally, lenses designed for use with your camera model and made by the same manufacturer will fit it. But don't overlook the lenses offered by the major independent lens manufacturers, such as Soligor, Spiratone, and Vivitar. They are often much lower in price and optically quite fine enough to produce good results in general nature work. One photographer went into a large New

York camera store intent on buying the telephoto lens made for his brand-new, famous-name camera. In addition to the brand-name lens, the salesman — a rare altruist — produced a similar lens from one of the independent lens makers. Not only did it fit the camera but a report by a major photo magazine rated it as nearly indistinguishable optically from the brand-name lens; and it cost only one-fourth as much. The photographer, dazzled by the report, handled both lenses. The salesman explained that through computer design and mass-production grinding methods, both lenses were fine pieces of optics. The more expensive lens was assembled and cemented a little more carefully than the cheaper one. "Aha," said the photographer, "when I drop it, it will fall apart." The salesman assured him that the second lens was cemented, just not quite as carefully as the first. And he could drop four of the cheaper lenses off the Empire State Building for the price of one bearing the brand name. The photographer bought the cheaper lens, pocketed the price difference, and is still more than satisfied some five years later.

Focal Length

The focal length of a lens controls both the magnification of the subject it will produce on your film and, by the same token, the angle of view it takes in. Most 35mm cameras come equipped with a "standard" or "normal" lens, 45mm to 55mm long (50mm = about 2"). (An 80mm lens is "normal" on 2¼" x 2¼" cameras.) The normal lens has an angle of view about 50 degrees and is widely useful in photographing landscapes or approachable living subjects.

There are, however, certain things a normal lens cannot do, as the emerging photographer will soon discover. The first time you photograph a graceful bird soaring overhead, only to discover the unimpressive speck on your negative or slide, you will feel the need of a long, or telephoto, lens. From a given camera-to-subject distance, the size of the image on the film is directly proportional to the focal length of the lens in use. Thus a 135mm lens will give you a subject image more than 2½ times the size of that given by your 50mm normal lens, and a 200mm will blow that distant bird or animal up to 4 times "normal" size.

Long lenses will overcome one basic problem of nature photography: distance. Designed for long-range shots, they will not focus on close distances, and have a restricted, narrow angle of view. For frame-filling shots made close up or for great expanses of landscape, you'll need a short-focal-length, wide-angle lens, which can focus at close distances and take in a wide field of view. The wide-angles for 35mm cameras come in focal lengths as short as 6mm, which gives a bizarre

Focal Length and Image Size

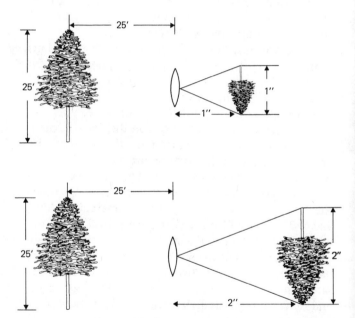

The size of an object as it appears on the film is directly related to the focal length of the lens when the camera-to-subject distance remains constant. In the drawings above, the subject is 25 feet tall and the camera-to-subject distance is a constant — 25 feet. The film-image size varies in direct proportion to the focal length of the lens in use.

fisheye perspective of the world. A wide-angle of 20mm or 21mm will be the widest you'll ever use for realistic nature shots. But for starters, the normal 50mm lens, plus a wide-angle of 35mm to 28mm and a telephoto of 135mm to 200mm, should enable you to deal with almost any subject your heart can desire or your imagination can contrive.

Lens "Speed"

The "speed" of a lens refers to its maximum opening or aperture — thus, the maximum amount of light it will admit. Engraved on the front of every lens is a cryptic but all important little ratio or fraction, for example, 1:2.8 or $f/2.8$. The second part, the number that changes from one lens to another, describes the capacity of the lens to admit light. It is expressed as a ratio or fraction because it refers to the relation between the maximum working diameter of the lens diaphragm and the focal length of the lens.

The photographic implications of the diaphragm and f/number will be explained in the section on *The Camera's Controls*. For the time being, we need consider them only in reference to the amount of light they admit. As the f/number is the bottom number of a fraction, the smaller it is, the larger the maximum diaphragm opening and the more light admitted. Some expensive, new 50mm lenses offer speeds of $f/1$ or even $f/.9$. They are treasures for the most extreme low-light work; but their high cost and the photographic problems they introduce make them an unwarranted extravagance for most photographers, and especially nature photographers.

There are practical limits to the maximum $f/$stop that can be designed into a lens. An $f/1$ 50mm lens would have to be 50mm in diameter, and an $f/1$ 200mm, 200mm in diameter. The amount of glass, optical corrections, and sheer weight and bulk of large-aperture long lenses make them a practical impossibility. Even with focal lengths where large apertures are optically and physically possible, they add immensely to the cost of the lens. For general daylight photography you'll probably never need a lens faster than a $f/2$ or $f/2.8$.

Like all the other features camera manufacturers offer, your primary question about super-speed lens should simply be, "Do I really need it?" If the answer is "no," you'll do well to buy a slower lens and invest your savings in higher quality, or some accessory more appropriate to your real needs.

"Automatic" Lenses

The diameter of your lens opening is adjustable, yet for viewing and focusing an SLR, the lens is best left wide open to admit the most light and help you see and focus sharply. With contemporary "automatic" lenses, the diaphragm stays wide open until you push your shutter release. Then it "stops down" automatically to the preselected f/stop before the picture is taken. After the exposure, the lens opens up all the way again. With old-fashioned, "manual" lenses, you must open the lens up each time, if you wish, for focusing, then stop it down before releasing the shutter. With more recent lenses of the "preset" design, the opening up and closing down is done with a ring that allows the manipulation without taking the camera away from your eye. And "semi-automatic" lenses allow you to open up the lens for focusing by pushing a lever on the lens barrel. The lens stops down to the preselected f/stop automatically when the shutter is released.

"Fully automatic" lenses offer you the brightest possible image for focusing and framing your shot without the bother of opening the diaphragm *and* remembering to close it back down for the exposure. Almost all standard lenses are now automatic, while many of the long focal lengths are still of the older design. Lens automation is a desirable feature, and having all your lenses operate in the same way is helpful in the quick, reflexive shooting so often necessary in nature photography.

Other Available Optics

Zoom Lenses

The zoom, or variable-focal-length, lenses designed for use with SLRs offer you the advantage of being able to vary the magnification of the image without moving the camera or changing lenses. Instead, you extend or retract the barrel of the lens; within, the optical elements shift to alter the focal length. You simly focus on your subject with the lens fully extended, then retract it until you have the composition you like. It's the lazy man's way, but it works. Zooms come in a variety of focal-length ranges — from 35mm-100mm to 200mm-600mm. The disadvantages of zoom lenses are their high price, size and weight, and optical quality somewhat less than equal to that of the better single-focal-length lenses. But zooms are especially useful in shooting color slides, where all cropping should be done in the camera. And if portability is a factor in the field, the flexibility of a single zoom lens is a real advantage.

Tele-Extenders

For distance work tele-extenders offer the possibility of increasing the focal length of the lenses you may already own. Tele-extenders are simple lenses that are inserted between your lens and camera body. Technically known as negative

lenses, they cause the light rays coming through
the lens to diverge, thereby enlarging the image.
Available in powers of 2x and 3x, they permit a
slight telephoto of 135mm to imitate a 270mm or
405mm. Tele-extenders can be used in combination to achieve greater power: a 2x plus a 3x would
provide a 5x increase in image size.

Although the good extenders are expensive, they
are certainly less costly than additional lenses, and
they can be used with all your lenses, giving you
many more focal lengths to work with. But the
image quality – the reason you invested in a good
lens to start out with – suffers. Beware of cheap
extenders unless an enlarged but poor image is
what you are after. Even with the best extenders
image quality is not what it would be if the photo
were taken with a good long lens. And with less
than the best extenders, the image can suffer a
serious loss of quality and clarity. Also, when the
image is enlarged by the extender, its brilliance is
reduced in the bargain. The reduction is proportional to the power of the extender *squared*. Thus,
that 5x image enlargement that sounded so attractive only sentences ago would reduce your image
brightness to 1/25 its normal strength and necessitate an exposure increase of 25x – 4½ *f*/stops.
And unless you have through-the-lens metering,
your exposures must be mentally recalculated to
take the extender into account.

Exposure Meters

Photographs of average subjects in average light conditions can be easily achieved by following basic exposures listed on the sheet that is enclosed with your film or through educated guesswork. By standardizing on certain favorite films, shooting a great deal under a variety of lighting conditions, and constantly criticizing your results, you will come to be able to make accurate exposure judgments for many lighting conditions. But for precise exposures, especially under tricky lighting conditions, use of a light meter may be necessary. Meters integrated into the viewing systems of modern cameras may seem the answer to a novice's prayer but occasionally they are not. And, the more complicated "center-weighted" or "balancing" through-the-lens meters may function perfectly but produce disastrous results. You must know how your light meter works in various circumstances.

Off-Camera, Hand-Held Meters

If your camera is not equipped with a meter, a hand-held meter should be your first accessory. And even if your camera features built-in metering, you probably should have a separate meter as a back-up, in case your built-in goes on the blink. There is also a large body of opinion to the effect that hand-held meters are the only serious kind. They can offer you added information and flexibility than the built-in type.

Light meters measure either reflected light or incident light. Reflected-light meters read the light coming from, or being reflected by, the subject. You merely aim the meter at the subject from the camera's point of view, and you have your reading. Special models with narrow angles of view – down to 1 degree – are available to take readings at a distance from small areas of the scene.

Incident-light meters measure the light falling directly on the subject. A light-collecting hemisphere is held so that the light falling on it is the same as the light falling on the subject. If the light at the camera position is the same as that striking the subject, all is well, and readings can be taken from the camera position. If either the camera or the subject is in shadow, the subject must be approached and a reading taken from the subject position with the hemisphere facing toward the camera. With unapproachable subjects, or high-contrast subjects that include both light and dark areas, the incident-light meter does not allow for the selective readings possible with the more popular reflected-light type – the photographer must learn to adjust the readings if he wishes to have detail in excessively light or dark areas of his photo.

Through-the-Lens Metering

Most SLRs now come equipped with built-in

reflected-light meters, which measure the light actually coming through the lens. Some take an average reading over the entire area of view; others emphasize the central portion of the field, on the theory that the main interest lies there. The center-weighted type of meter allows for selective reading and exposure to compensate for overly bright or dark areas of your photographs. With either type, simply by turning the lens-diaphragm ring or shutter-speed dial to center an arrow or needle in the viewer, a correct general exposure can be obtained.

Meter Calibration

As ingenious as reflected-light meters might seem, they are deceptively single-minded. They are calibrated to translate a single luminance area from intensity into exposure and will produce an average gray tone in a photograph. Photographically, "average" means a tone that reflects precisely 18 per cent of the light falling on it. The meter doesn't know what your intentions are, though you presumably do. No matter what, the meter will indicate an exposure to reproduce the average of the subject as just that 18 per cent gray tone. If your subject is more or less average, with some dark areas, some light, and some in-between, the meter's reading will result in a well-balanced exposure.

Exposure Meter Types

An incident-light meter

A reflected light meter

A spot meter

A Support for Your Camera

The extra weight and bulk of a tripod or other camera support may seem more than you can bear, especially on a pack trip or long hike; but the extra baggage is well worth its weight. A tripod is a must for any time or slow shutter exposure. There are many photographers, including professionals, who cannot successfully hand hold an exposure longer than 1/15th of a second. Some have trouble at 1/125th. Even if your hand is as steady as a surgeon's, the stability of the tripod affords you the luxury of being able to view and crop carefully, to level horizons, and to avoid that extraneous element, be it animal, vegetable, or a telephone pole poking in from the side of your photo. Even a tripod-mounted camera is subject to motion. Tripods have a "moment" — a vibration period which is independent of their weight or basic stability. After you have framed and focused, you would do well to use a cable release to disturb the set up as little as possible during exposure.

Lenses longer than 135mm, in particular, require steady support even at high shutter speeds. The camera is thrown off balance by the extra weight at the front, making it hard to hold steadily by hand. At the same time the magnification that brings the distant subject up close also magnifies any jiggle or jerk that punctuates your picture taking. For action work, there are camera supports

that offer increased stability without the rigidity of
a tripod. A monopod is a single-legged support that
is simply braced against the ground, allowing the
camera to be swung in an arc to follow the action.
A shoulder pod, resembling a rifle stock, is braced
against the shoulder for support. Even a small
table-top tripod, or lowpod, can be braced against
the chest for steadiness. The Rowi clamp, basically
an ordinary C-clamp with a camera mount attached, allows you to fix the camera to anything
from a tree branch to a car door.

Miscellaneous Equipment

Beyond the basics — cameras, lenses, meters — the
equipment you assemble should bear the stamp of
your personal shooting needs. For close-up work a
supplementary light source — a simple flash gun or
flash-cube attachment, or a sophisticated self-set-
ting electronic flash, or strobe — is often useful.
Inexpensive close-up lenses permit you to work at
short distances with your normal lens. Cable and
air-pressure releases allow you to trigger the shutter
without shaking the camera. Remote releases activated by your subject, or by you from a distance,
are used for animal candid shots. These and other
special accessories, both photographic and non-
photographic, will be discussed in the appropriate
chapters later in the book.

Caring for Your Equipment – An Ounce of Prevention

Your camera is a precision machine, and its lens is a carefully designed and manufactured optical system. They must be respected and cared for as such. So, the best prescription for the care and feeding of your equipment is the proverbial ounce of prevention.

Maintenance

The primary rule of equipment care is simple: keep it clean. Accumulated dust and grit can stall the operation of the finest camera, and a dirty lens, no matter how much you paid for it, will produce only smudgy pictures.

The case designed for your camera will go a long way toward protecting it from grime. A so-called ever-ready case, with a removable front, allows you to keep the camera cased while shooting. You need remove it only to load and unload (not in the midst of a dust storm, please). And when you're shooting in foul and foggy weather, a plastic bag with a hole cut out for the lens makes an ideal raincoat to protect the camera from dampness and possible corrosion. Suited-up, the camera can withstand the elements as long as you can.

If the camera still gets damp somehow, dry it out as soon as possible. A blower-type hairdryer is an easy solution. One former *Life* staff photographer claims to have relied on daily hairdryer sessions plus a weekly oven-drying to protect his equipment while on assignment in the tropics. For less exotic locales, you need only consider the hairdryer therapy.

"Damp" does not mean immersed in water. If your camera gets drowned, the best advice is to keep it in water to prevent the air from rusting it until you can get the poor machine to a qualified repairman. You may feel entirely ridiculous returning from a shooting with camera in a pail or plastic bag full of water, but it is the only remedy for your predicament. If corrosion sets in before the camera is taken apart, dried, and reassembled, there will be little hope of bringing it back to life. Even with the best professional help, which is bound to be very expensive, the prognosis is not good. Perhaps the kindest suggestion is that if you insist on dropping your camera into the lake – or, worse yet, the saline sea – you might as well resign yourself to buying a new one.

Dirt, the eternal enemy, is more easily dealt with. For prevention, keep your camera cased and even in a plastic bag when not in use. An inexpensive blower-brush — with soft bristles and a rubber squeeze-ball to provide a squirt of air — will blow dust away. Pressure cans filled with freon are now available to provide a dry, purifying blast. A little distilled water or lens cleaner applied with the lens tissue or a gentle wipe with an often-washed, lint-free linen handkerchief will keep your front and rear lens elements clean. Don't overdo. Lenses should not be drenched with cleaning solutions. Liquid can seep in around the edge of the elements and dissolve the cement that holds them in place. Many photographers equip each lens with a clear skylight or ultraviolet filter for protection. Cleaning a filter requires less care than cleaning a lens, and replacing a scratched or damaged filter is certainly less expensive than replacing a lens.

Necessarily, you'll visit your camera repairman whenever your camera breaks down. But, as with the dentist, you should visit the camera "doctor" more often than disaster necessitates. Outside of larger cities, finding a competent repair shop may prove difficult. Many manufacturers accept their equipment for mail-order repair, but this takes time. For local repair, inquire about service from a local pro.

Your camera should be cleaned and checked periodically to keep it in optimum working order. A good professional repairman has diagnostic machines and procedures that can check shutter speeds, focus, synchronization, and other features quickly and exactly, saving you the sad experience of discovering your camera's malfunction in those pictures you worked so hard to get. A professional check-up should be a matter of course before any special photographic trip or expedition. If time does not permit, or if you must cut corners economically, be sure to expose a roll of film at various shutter-speed/lens-opening combinations and have it processed to check the camera's performance beforehand.

Safety

While traveling, protect your camera against unnecessary hazards. Never keep it in the glove compartment or trunk of a car to rattle and bump around and bake; or lying loose on the seat or back window shelf where a sudden stop can send it flying. If you are driving with only your camera and one lens along, place them, out of the way, on the floor on some soft cushioning material. If you're transporting your entire kit, place it flat on the floor. Never leave a camera or camera case in a parked car. Theft, alas, is as much a threat to equipment safety as dropping, drowning, and dirt. If you travel by plane, *never* surrender your equipment case to luggage handlers. Despite airline assurances, both in person and in their advertisements, and the "fragile" stickers they'll offer to put on your case, airlines treat luggage less delicately than precision optical equipment requires. Insist on taking your camera case along with you and stow it under the seat or at your feet.

An insurance policy might someday prove to be the most valuable photo accessory that you own. Policies are readily available and are not too expensive — especially when the policy's cost is compared with what it would run for you to replace your equipment. Discuss policies with an insurance broker or agent and make sure that the one you choose covers your equipment away from home and for damage and loss as well as theft.

A Carrying Case

Commercially available equipment cases come in a variety of designs and materials — from aluminum through leather — and price ranges from cheap to expensive. In choosing one, consider (within your budget, of course) three aspects: protection, longevity, and expansion. The case should be sturdy enough to offer some insulation from weather and hard knocks. (A white case will reflect heat rather than transmitting it to its valuable contents.) It should be well made to assure long use without repair to straps, handles, locks, or hinges. It should be large enough to allow room to include the extra equipment and accessories you'll doubtless find yourself buying and using. Finding a carrying case is strangely one of the most personal areas of equipment choice. Airline bags (preferably from the more exotic airlines), waterproof game bags, army-surplus and Boy Scout backpacks, specially fitted attaché cases and suitcases, and even styrofoam picnic hampers are used as camera cases by top professionals. As you please, but, please do consider the well-made, sturdy cases that have been professionally designed to protect your equipment.

Packing Your Case

For traveling, pack your case with an eye toward protection. Many of the commercially available cases come with foam filling that can be cut to cradle each piece of equipment. If your case came without such insulation, buy some foam and cut it to fit into the case and around your camera and lenses. Or use their original styrofoam packing. The lens should be removed from the camera body. An inexpensive body cap will seal the lens mount. Lenses should be capped both fore and aft, and foam-lined leather or leatherlike lens cases are a good investment for safety. For working, your case should be packed so as to allow quick and handy retrieval of the equipment you want, when you want it. Organization is the first word. Work out a system that works for you.

A case that proves perfect for travel may also prove entirely inappropriate to your needs in the field. If your camera and equipment are to remain safe and secure on a cross-country hike, in a boat, or even while you ski from here to there, you may want to integrate them into a backpack. Cameras travel quite well along with your other gear if you take the care to insulate them by wrapping them in a sweater or piece of foam rubber, with a stout rubber band around the whole thing. Camping stores offer a grand selection of field packs for the imaginative photographer. A pack with many small exterior pouches helps in keeping such smaller accessories as filters, spare lens caps, films and lens shades safe, sorted, and easily at hand. Small belt pouches are ideal for a camera with lens, extra lenses, and a supply of film.

Films and Filters

Pity the poor nature photographer of a century ago who needed to tote a complete darkroom into the field, where he laboriously coated fragile glass plates with mildly light-sensitive concoctions of his own devising and developed his exposures on the spot. Today, the assortment of different films, their dependable high quality, increased light sensitivity, and wide availability in popular sizes, gives you a seemingly limitless — and confusing — range of choices. If you consider your photographic plans in advance, you can choose a film that has been tailored specifically for the subject you intend to photograph, the working situation, and the end purpose to which you hope to put the results. But for general work, the most practical answer to the bewildering array of available films is to find one you like and stick with it. As your familiarity with the film increases, so will your creative possibilities for using it.

Filters will extend the performance characteristics of your film in predictable ways if you know how to use them. Their applications will be considered in the second section of this chapter. Filters are often used, or misused, to create exaggerated visual effects — midnight skies at noon, purple snowscapes, blazing sunsets. The bias of this handbook is that in most cases nature is "creative" enough to be photographed in its own image with the emphasis on realistic or naturalistic results and without too much additional "creativity" on the part of the photographer. We will consider only the general technical aspects of filters here, and cover their specialized – and judicious – applications in later chapters.

Films

Films vary in quality and photographic characteristics among brands and types. Fortunately, top-quality, brand-name films are widely available in most popular sizes – though, just to be sure, it's a good idea to take along a supply of your favorite if you plan to be far from your proven source. There's no avoiding the plain fact that almost anywhere in the world, and certainly anywhere in the United States, Kodak dominates the film field. It's a pretty sure bet that if a local dispensary doesn't have the type and size of film you want in the distinctive yellow package, they won't have it at all. This is not to deny the fact that other brands, such as GAF, Ilford, Fuji, and Agfa, produce perfectly good products, with their own useful and attractive photographic characteristics. They simply aren't as widely available as Kodak films, and if you want to standardize for the sake of consistency and self-assurance (a good idea), Kodak films are the practical choice. Fortunately, in this case at least, Kodak's near-monopoly goes hand in hand with quality and dependability, so you can accept the inevitable with good grace.

Even after you've chosen an appropriate film and exposed it correctly, processing and printing can still be a problem, turning triumph into disaster. Kodak offers processing services for its own color films, and it does a clean, reliable job with highly automated equipment. For Kodak color films, such as Kodacolor, Ektachrome, and Ektacolor, which can be over- and underdeveloped to compensate for exposure problems, you may want to use an independent processor — likewise for all black-and-white films, which the manufacturer does not handle. The choice of a lab is vital. If you're serious about your work, there's no point in taking your exposed film to the corner drugstore to be sent to some mass-processing outfit. Many of them almost guarantee mediocre results from even the best exposures. If you aren't set up with the equipment and don't have the patience to process your own film — and it requires some care and practice to do it right every time — then find a good custom lab to do it for you. It won't cost that much more, and the results will be worth the difference.

Film Characteristics

Film speed: The so-called speed of a film is a measure of its sensitivity to light. The common American film-speed rating system was developed by the *A*merican *S*tandards *A*ssociation (now the American National Standards Institute) and is expressed in ASA numbers. Under the ASA arithmetic system, a doubling of the rating indicates a doubling of the film's sensitivity to light. Thus, in a given light situation, a film rated at ASA 200 needs only ½ the exposure of a film rated at ASA 100 to yield an image of the same density. The common European system, DIN (*D*eutsche *I*ndustrie *N*orm), uses a logarithmic progression – an increase of 3 indicates a doubling of film sensitivity.

The film speed ratings given by the manufacturers are conservative. They assume average subjects and normal exposure and processing. With many black-and-white and a few color films, *effective* speeds can be doubled or even tripled by "pushing" with special developers or by increased developing times and/or temperatures. But these techniques should remain emergency measures and can often be overcome by thoughtful film choice and well thought-out exposures. For the sake of image quality it is best to choose a film of sufficient speed to satisfy the conditions of light and subject you expect to encounter and to expose it according to standard recommendations. For not only does film speed indicate light sensitivity, it is also related to grain and contrast characteristics that greatly affect how your final picture will look and continual use of over- or mis-rated films will bring worse confusion than incessantly jumping from one film to another.

Contrast: A film's "contrast" refers to the tonal range it is able to reproduce correctly. Most medium-speed films have normal contrast: when properly exposed and processed, they represent the tonal values of the subject pretty much as perceived by the eye. Slow, low-ASA films tend to be of higher contrast; fast films, of lower contrast — the opposite tends to be true of color film. Most popular films combine medium speed with normal contrast, and they will produce good results with average subjects under average conditions. If, however, you want to photograph a high-contrast subject, with overly bright highlights and deep shadows, you'll get better results with a low-contrast film. And conversely, a higher-contrast film can be used to add some zip to less contrasting subjects, such as those photographed on a shadowless, overcast day. And, post-exposure processing adjustments can be used to adjust the contrast of any film.

Grain: The light-sensitive emulsion of the film contains tiny particles of silver. Transformed by exposure to light into a "latent image," and then darkened by the processing chemicals, these silver particles combine to make up the image.

Even in fast emulsions the grain structure is invisible to the unaided eye. But when your negative is enlarged or your transparency projected, the magnified grains appear as a sandy, granular texture. Under moderate enlargement, viewed from a normal distance, the grain is hardly noticeable. But, especially if you plan to make large prints, the best rule is to choose a film only as fast as you need and expose and develop it according to the manufacturer's advice.

For the sake of avoiding both excessive grain and contrast, don't try to push the film beyond its rated speed by overprocessing unless you have to or unless you want to create some special effect. The more you develop your film, the more the silver in the exposed areas will darken, while the less-exposed areas remain relatively unaffected. The result is increased contrast between light and dark areas in the image. At the same time increased development tends to make the silver particles clump together, producing a visible grain pattern.

Which Film?

All ordinary black-and-white films yield negatives, from which final prints are made. Their differences are in film speed — and, by the same token, in contrast and grain. For action or low-light shooting a "fast" film of ASA 400 or higher, such as Kodak's Tri-X or Ilford HP4 is indicated; slower films of ASA 25 to 125, such as Kodak's Panatomic-X rated at ASA 32, or Plus-X or Ilford FP4, rated at 125, can be used for static landscapes and still-lifes where their fine-grain detail is welcome. Many professional photographers rely on higher speed films for their general work. The need to get a usable picture at any cost in image quality, along with the fact that increased grain (along with detail and tonal quality) is lost in most media reproduction, tempts the pros to rely on a fast film as their all-'round shooting stock. Even at the cost of some extra bulk in the field, and the extra problem of keeping his inventory straight, the nature photographer may want to expand his options to include two or three films of varying speeds: Panatomic-X (ASA 25) perhaps, for fine-grain, slow-speed work; Tri-X (ASA 400) for action shots; and Plux-X (ASA 125) for everything in-between.

In choosing a color film, you have to think ahead to the end product you want. "Reversal" films (most with names ending in "chrome," such as Kodachrome, Ektachrome, Agfachrome, Fujichrome), will be returned to you as slides, to be looked at with a projector or a hand viewer. Color "negative" films, such as Kodacolor, Ektacolor,

Agfacolor, GAF Color Print Film, produce negatives, from which prints are made. Slides can be made into prints, but a negative must be made first, at extra expense and loss of image quality. So, choose accordingly.

Film Care

Film packages carry expiration dates for your information and protection. Avoid buying films that are outdated, or nearly so, even at reduced prices. Any film emulsion is a sophisticated chemical compound; it remains stable for a long time, but not forever. The expiration date is the manufacturer's warning that standard performance can no longer be assured. Perfect pictures can be produced on expired films – sometimes. But a film that you cannot depend on is a very poor bargain. Buy current films in quantities sufficient for your foreseeable needs.

Beyond age, moisture and heat are the main threats to standard film performance. Films are now packaged in moisture-proof foil or handy little aluminum or plastic cans. Keep them in their original wrappers until you're ready to use them, and return them to the package or some other moisture-proof container after exposure.

Dampness is insidious. You may well become accustomed to the high humidity on a tropical shooting trip, or find the morning and evening fogs and mists of an oceanside locale picturesque, but your film, alas, will do neither. Even if stashed away someplace, it will not be safe from moisture unless you deliberately make it so. A plastic-lidded coffee can loaded with your exposed film *and* a small packet or perforated container of silica gel, a desiccant available from chemical dealers, will serve as a moisture-proof film safe. The efficacy of the silica gel should be renewed often by a thorough drying in a hot oven.

Heat is a more obvious hazard. If you're hot, so is your film. Indoors, store film in some cool spot, or for the long term, in the refrigerator. When you step out from your air-conditioned home or hotel, or when you remove the film from the refrigerator, you must allow the *sealed* package and its contents to warm up before opening. Otherwise moisture from the warm air will condense on the cold film. Once outdoors, protect your loaded camera and extra film supply from the sun. High temperature will raise the effective speed of your film and affect the color rendition in your color work. Have your exposed films processed as soon as possible. Damage can occur after exposure as well as before.

Low temperature will also affect the perform-ance of your film. Prolonged exposure to freezing temperatures will lower the effective ASA. Cold will make the film brittle, increasing the risk of it snapping if advanced too quickly. Static electricity can also occur from a too-quick film advance in low temperatures; it will not alter the performance of your film but will mar your pictures with lightninglike flashes of light.

The best defense against the cold is simple enough: keep your camera and film as warm as possible while working. The loaded camera should be carried inside your parka or coat, where it will be warmed by body heat. Extra rolls of film should be carried in pants, jacket, or sweater pockets to keep them as close to your warming body as possible.

Filters

"Photography" literally means drawing with light. And nature photography usually implies photography with existing or available light — the kind nature provides. For realistic, natural-looking photographs, a good panchromatic black-and-white film or daylight color film will usually record your subjects just as you would have them if you have visualized the image before exposure. But occasionally you may wish to adjust the light and the resulting color or tonal balance of your picture. This is often the case with scenic photography, and the use of filters is given special attention in the chapter on *Landscapes*.

Natural daylight appears colorless, or "white,"

to the viewer except very early or late in the day. However, it is made up of different wavelengths of light, each of which, if seen in isolation, appears a different color. Witness the many-colored constituents of daylight when it is broken down into its various wavelengths and colors, from red through violet, in a rainbow or passing through a prism. Everything absorbs certain of the colors from the light falling on it and reflects back others. The portion and amount of light it reflects gives the subject its particular color and tonality. Filters, too, absorb some wavelengths of the spectrum and pass others, according to their apparent colors. Thus, they alter the color and tonal values of a

The Electromagnetic Spectrum

Cosmic rays	Gamma rays		Ultra-violet rays	WHITE LIGHT		Short Hertzian waves	Radio waves and long electrical oscillations
	← X-rays →				Infra-red rays		

The full spectrum contains everything from cosmic rays through radio waves.

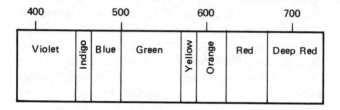

**The Visible Spectrum —
White Light**

| 400 | | 500 | | 600 | | 700 |

| Violet | Indigo | Blue | Green | Yellow | Orange | Red | Deep Red |

The portion of the electromagnetic spectrum visible to the human eye includes wavelengths from about 400 millimicrons (violet) through about 700 millimicrons (red).

photographic image by holding back part of the light spectrum reflected from the subject through the lens and onto the film. Generally, a filter can be depended on to transmit its own color (rendering objects of that color lighter than normal in the final print or transparency) and to stop its complementary color (making it darker than normal in the result). Thus, a red filter will pass red and stop blue and green.

In the process of passing only part of the spectrum, the filter stops some of the total light from your subject before it reaches the film. To compensate for this loss of light intensity, an exposure increase is necessary. If the camera has a built-in meter behind the lens — thus, behind the

How Filters Work

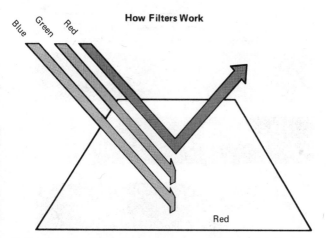

Reflection: An object is seen as being whatever color it reflects most. Other colors are absorbed.

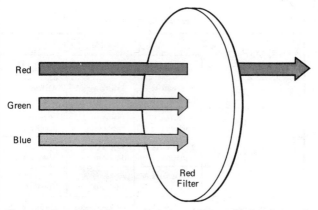

Transmission: Depending on its color, a filter will absorb certain colors and pass others.

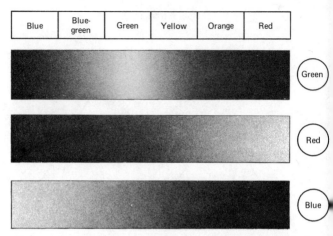

| Blue | Blue-green | Green | Yellow | Orange | Red |

Degree of transmission and absorption: A filter will transmit a maximum amount of its own color, absorb its neighboring colors in the spectrum somewhat, and absorb its complementary color most.

Practical filter effects

COLOR OF FILTER	COLOR IN SCENE		
	RED	GREEN	BLUE
YELLOW	Transmits & lightens	Transmits & lightens	Absorbs & darkens
GREEN	Absorbs & darkens	Transmits & lightens	Absorbs & darkens
ORANGE	Transmits & lightens	Absorbs & darkens	Absorbs & darkens
RED	Transmits & lightens	Absorbs & darkens	Absorbs & darkens
BLUE	Absorbs & darkens	Absorbs & darkens	Transmits & lightens

filter as well — mental calculations are often overlooked, since the decreased light intensity will be taken into account somewhat in the meter reading. But, for scrupulously correct exposures, an unfiltered reading should be taken and the exposure adjustment indicated by the filter factor applied. The accompanying chart lists filter factors — the necessary exposure increases from various colors and densities of filters. Applying these factors is absolutely imperative if your camera lacks a built-in, through-the-lens meter. They are also useful in deciding beforehand what speed film you will need if you plan to shoot a whole roll of filtered shots. And, as mentioned above, they should be applied independently to unfiltered, through-the-lens readings.

Filters for Black-and-White Photography

Modern, general-purpose panchromatic films are sensitive to all colors of light. They reduce the multicolored world to tones of gray more or less proportional to the brightness of the different areas of the subject. The problem is that, except for some color-blind people, most of us, including photographers, do not see in tones of gray. The bright red flowers on a healthy green bush will stand out in vivid contrast. Translated into a black-and-white photograph, however, the flowers and leaves may well reflect nearly the same

Suggested Exposure Increase Factors
for use with Panchromatic Films

Filter color	Exposure factor
Light yellow	1.5
Medium yellow	2
Light green	4
Dark green	5
Deep yellow or orange	3
Medium red	8
Blue	5

Filter Conversion Table

Filter factor (x)	f/stop without filter is:							
	2.8	3.5	4.5	5.6	6.3	8	11	16
	f/stop with filter:							
1.5	2.3	2.9	3.7	4.6	5.1	6.6	9.2	13.0
2	2.0	2.5	3.2	4.0	4.5	5.6	8.0	11.0
2.5	1.8	2.2	2.8	3.6	4.0	5.2	7.1	10.1
3	1.6	2.0	2.6	3.3	3.6	4.6	6.6	9.2
4	1.4	1.7	2.2	2.8	3.2	4.0	5.6	8.0
5	—	1.6	2.0	2.5	2.9	3.6	5.0	7.0
6	—	1.4	1.8	2.3	2.6	3.3	4.5	6.6
7	—	1.3	1.7	2.1	2.4	3.0	4.2	6.1
8	—	—	1.6	2.0	2.2	2.8	4.0	5.6
10	—	—	1.4	1.8	2.0	2.5	3.5	5.0

The filter factor conversion table is designed to allow you to take unfiltered exposure readings and then to apply the necessary exposure increase without resorting to mental calculations. It is for use with both color and black-and-white films. For exact exposures, *do not* rely on through-the-lens readings made through your filter. And, *do not* reset hand-held meters at a lower ASA because a filter is in use. Instead, take unfiltered readings at the proper ASA and use the chart.

amounts of their different light wavelengths, and appear as almost indistinguishable shades of gray in the print. A picture that depends on color contrast for its dazzle may well come out as an undistinguished gray blot in black and white. Previewing your subject through a Wratten #90 Viewing Filter will suggest the tonal values you can expect if the subject is to be photographed on unfiltered panchromatic film.

A contrast filter can often improve your black-and-white photos. For instance, in the case cited above, a red filter could be used to stop the green light being reflected from the leaves, making them significantly darker than the flowers in the picture; or a green filter could be used to stop the red light from the flowers, making them darker than the leaves. In either case, the filter would be used to increase tonal contrast, which is the basic vocabulary of black-and-white photography.

Black-and-white results sometimes fail to live up to expectations due to differences between the color sensitivity of the human eye and film. The eye is most sensitive to yellow, the first color we come to see as infants. The film, alas, does not share the eye's positive prejudice toward yellow and complementary bias against blue. Wordsworth's "sprightly" daffodils would not do well in unfiltered black-and-white photography. The flowers would be reproduced as a less-than-dazzling mid-gray in the picture, and the blue sky might well be washed out. Happily, the disagreement between eye and film can be resolved with a single filter. A yellow filter will maintain the perky yellow highlights which the eye leads us to expect, while holding back the blue light from the sky.

Filters for Color Photography

Filters for use with color films are much less deeply tinted and much more subtle in effect than the contrast filters used in black-and-white photography. Yet they can play a useful role in securing naturalistic, pleasing color rendition and correcting the slight color imbalances that occur in natural daylight.

Light-balancing filters subtly adjust the overall tone of a color photograph. A pale-blue filter will cool the general reddishness of photos taken at sunrise or sunset, whereas a light red will warm up exposures taken in the bluish light of an overcast day, or of subjects in shadow.

A pale-pink skylight filter or a yellowish haze filter will have an effect similar to that of the warming red light-balancing filter; a seemingly colorless ultraviolet filter will stop ultraviolet rays, which are invisible to the eye but lend a blue cast to distant shots. Color-compensating (CC) filters are pale, tinted gelatin squares in varying intensities of cyan, magenta, and yellow, used to correct color balance in transparencies for reproduction. CC filters can be bound right into your slide mount to correct the color for projection and display. They can also be placed over the lens for use in shooting, but they damage easily, so their utility in the field is limited.

Other Filters

Two filters used in both black-and-white and color photography have little effect on the color of the light reaching the film. The neutral density filter simply reduces the amount of light, affecting all colors equally. It comes in handy when you are loaded with fast film in bright light, or when you want to use a slow shutter speed and/or large aperture that would otherwise result in overexposure.

The polarizing screen, or polarizing filter, is used to eliminate reflections and glare from the subject in just the same way as polarizing sunglasses do. Ordinarily, lightwaves vibrate in many directions along their axis of travel. Polarized light, which causes reflection and glare, vibrates in only one plane. The polarizing filter is incised overall with a screen of fine lines. It can be rotated over the lens until it blocks all or some of the polarized light coming from the subject. The effect can be observed in the SLR viewfinder. With a rangefinder camera, the filter must be held up to the eye and

Neutral Density Filters
(Transmission and Exposure Factor Table)

Density	Percent of Trans- mission	Approximate Fraction of Light Passed	Approxi- mate Increase in Stops	Approximate Equivalent Filter Factor
0.10	80	4/5	1/3	1.25
0.20	63	2/3	2/3	1.6
0.30	50	1/2	1	2.
0.40	40	2/5	1-1/3	2.5
0.50	32	1/3	1-2/3	3.1
0.60	25	1/4	2	4.
0.70	20	1/5	2-1/3	5.
0.80	16	1/6	2-2/3	6.3
0.90	13	1/8	3	7.9
1.00	10	1/10	3-1/3	10
2.00	1.	1/100	6-2/3	100
3.00	0.10	1/1,000	10	1000
4.00	0.010	1/10,000	13-1/2	10,000

Neutral density filters are available in a great range of densities. A 0.10 will transmit 4/5 of the available light and necessitate an exposure increase of only 1/2 stop while a 4.00 will transmit only 1/10,000th of the light and call for an exposure increase of 13½ stops. The chart above can be used two ways. Obviously, it will give you your exposure increase factor when a certain neutral density filter is in use. Or, if a certain unfiltered exposure is indicated and you wish to open your lens up or slow your shutter, the chart can show you which filter to use.

How a Polarizing Filter Works

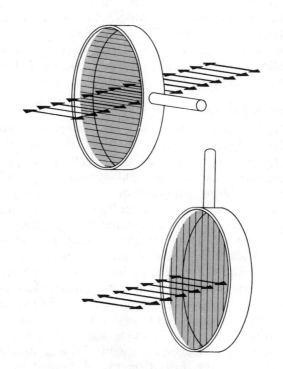

Polarized light vibrates in only one plane. When the polarizing filter is aligned, as it is in the top drawing, polarized light passes right through. When the filter is rotated so that its fine grid is at right angles to the plane of the polarized light (bottom drawing), it stops the polarized light effectively.

rotated until the desired effect is achieved. It is then mounted on the lens in that position of rotation. In nature photography the polarizing filter is effective in reducing the glare in seascapes and seeing through the surface reflections on shallow pools of water. In general use the polarizing filter tends to make colors richer and deeper.

Care and Handling of Filters

Filters come in different forms — from simple gelatin squares to gelatin between glass to color-tinted glass. The gelatins, or "gels," are the least expensive. They can be held or taped in front of the lens during exposure or fitted into a special filter holder attached to your lens. The color-tinted glass filters are the most expensive, but they are less vulnerable to scratching and damage than the gels. They are carefully ground so as not to compromise the optical performance of your lens. Filters are available from your camera manufacturer or from independents such as Tiffen and Spiratone. Usually, you pay a premium for the famous-name brand, without any too significant increase in photographic quality. Mounted filters must cover the full diameter of your lens, so choose carefully.

Any filter must be kept scrupulously clean. There's not much point in improving the tonal or color rendition of your picture if, in the bargain, you fuzz it up by placing a dirty or marred filter in front of the lens. Gelatin filters should be handled only by the edges to avoid scratches and finger-prints; they should be dusted lightly after use and kept in their envelopes when not in use to avoid fading. Glass filters — whether the gelatin-be-tween-glass or tinted-glass type — can be cleaned with lens cleaner solution or distilled water. Beware of any liquid seeping in around the edges of the sandwich-type filter; the binding glue can be dissolved, and the colored layer spotted or marred around the edge.

The Camera's Controls

Two controls, basic to all adjustable cameras, allow you to vary your exposures according to the light conditions and the sensitivity of the film you have chosen. Whether you follow the general guide packed with your film, or the more precise advice of a light meter, exposure is directly related to both the shutter speed and lens aperture. These two controls adjust the duration and the intensity of light entering your camera. Exposure is the product of the two factors. By increasing one and decreasing the other, the exposure can be kept constant, and you will get images of identical density.

The particular combination you choose will determine the quality of the resulting image. This chapter will explain both the shutter and lens settings, their interrelationship, and the pictorial effects they will produce. The focusing adjustment on your camera will also be covered.

Shutter Speed

The camera's shutter speeds — the speeds at which the camera's shutter mechanism can be made to open and close — are designated in seconds and fractions thereof, usually ranging from 1 second through 1/500th or 1/1000th of a second. Each setting represents one half of the preceding mark. By going from 1/50th second to 1/100th second you'll halve the interval during which light is permitted to strike your film. It's as simple as that.

Aperture

The lens of your camera contains an adjustable diaphragm made up of overlapping metal leaves. By turning a ring on the lens barrel you can adjust the diaphragm to dilate or contract the lens opening, or iris. The larger the opening, of course, the more light admitted.

Lens settings are commonly known as f/stops, and unlike the orderly arithmetic progression of shutter-speed settings, the f/stops indicated on your lens may prove confusing at first.

Each f/stop is arrived at by some simple mathematics. The formula is:

$$\frac{1}{f} = \frac{\text{aperture diameter}}{\text{focal length}}$$

For example, an f/stop of 2 on a 50mm lens indicates an aperture 25mm in diameter; while the same $f/2$ on a 100mm lens produces an aperture of 50mm. Under the same lighting conditions, the $f/2$

stop on either lens results in the same amount of light reaching the film.

Imagine a room with the sun streaming straight through a window with a diffusing curtain in one wall. The window represents the diaphragm opening; the opposite wall, the film. If the wall is 8 feet from the window, a certain amount of the sunlight, x, will reach it. If the wall is 16 feet away — 2 times as far — it will get only 1/4 as much light. This is known as the inverse square law: double the distance, quarter the intensity of the light. For an equal amount of light to reach the wall at the doubled distance, the window area would have to be 4 times as large. Likewise, given the same light conditions, a lens with a focal length of 100mm needs an aperture 4 times as large as a 50mm lens to deliver the same amount of light to the film plane.

The numerical progression of f/stops is not a neat arithmetic sequence of doubling and halving. Just as with the window, light is entering your lens over the *area* of the aperture you have selected. Remember that the f/stop relates to the diameter of the opening and that the area of a circle is calculated by squaring its radius (d/2). Doubling the diameter will not admit twice as much light to enter — it will admit 4 times as much light.

The markings on your lens indicate a physical progression of apertures which allows for halving

Aperture Diameter and Light Transmission

If the mathematical basis for the squaring and doubling principle of aperture settings eludes you, perhaps the drawings above will help. In both drawings, the square has a side measuring "d." In the first drawing "d" also serves as the diameter of the circle. In the second drawing, each circle has a diameter of 1/2 "d" and an area 1/4 that of the larger circle.

or doubling the amount of light entering. The range is usually 1, 1.4, 2, 2.8, 4, 5.6, 8, 11, 16, 22. Remember, too, that f/stops are fractions $\left(\dfrac{1}{f} = \dfrac{d}{f}\right)$. Thus, f/4, representing an aperture with a diameter of 1/4 the focal length of the lens, is smaller than f/2 – 1/2 of the focal length. The larger the f/ number the smaller the aperture and the less light admitted. A setting of f/1 would admit more than 500 times more light than a setting of f/22.

Exposure Control

The exposure readings given by your meter or exposure tables indicate a starting point. Exposures of $f/11$ at 1/125th, $f/8$ at 1/250th, or $f/5.6$ at 1/500th of a second, and so on up and down the f/stop and shutter-speed scales, will all give equivalent exposures in terms of total light — intensity times duration. The aperture size grows as the exposure time diminishes. But, choosing the best combination of f/stop and shutter speed for the picture you want to make is more than a matter of light measurement. A photograph taken at a large aperture and fast shutter speed will prove entirely different visually from the same composition taken at a small aperture and slower shutter speed. You can easily demonstrate this point for yourself. Using a single subject, make a sequence of exposures going from the largest aperture and fastest shutter-speed combination that the light permits to the smallest aperture and slowest shutter-speed combination. The results will speak for themselves. The following section will discuss the causes for the differences that will be apparent in such a sequence of pictures.

Choosing a Shutter Speed

The speed of whatever action or movement may be taking place in the scene you wish to shoot is the first consideration in determining the appropriate shutter speed. Photographing a cheetah or deer running at full tilt will obviously necessitate a fast shutter speed. But so will photographing a close-up of a wildflower swaying gently in the breeze. The speed of your subject's motion must be considered in relation to its size in the viewfinder. Indeed, the distant, racing cheetah may require exactly the same shutter setting to stop its motion as the far slower-moving, but closer, wildflower.

The direction of motion is the third consideration for choosing a speed. If a subject is moving directly toward or away from you, its movement is less apparent than if it is moving across your field of view. In technical terms, the image is displaced less. Thus, it's easier to get an unblurred shot of a rhino charging straight at you — to "stop" him, at least on film — than of one running past, if it's any consolation. It may be your last picture, but it won't be blurred.

Equivalent Exposures — Different Results (overleaf)

The look of two photographs will be altered dramatically between a large-aperture fast-shutter exposure and a small-aperture slow-shutter exposure. The two photos on the following pages were both shot with a 58mm lens focused at 15 feet. The apertures and shutter speeds used were adjusted in combination to produce equivalent exposures. In the first photo, the branch across the top of the picture is sharp but little else is. This photo was made at an aperture setting of f/2.8. In the second photo, both the branch and a good deal more of the surrounding landscape are in focus. It was taken at an aperture setting of f/11. Photos by Rafael Fraguada.

Choosing an F/Stop

If you hope to freeze fast action with a high shutter speed, a wide-open f/stop will be dictated by the need to give an adequate exposure. But when stopping action is not the prime consideration, your choice of aperture will depend more on the photographic effect you want.

The f/stop does more than control the amount of light that reaches the film. As the accompanying photographs illustrate, an increase in the size of the aperture decreases the depth of the area in your field of view that will appear in acceptably sharp focus in the photograph. This zone of sharpness is called the depth of field. Markings on the lens barrel indicate the depth of field at each f/stop for any camera-to-subject distance.

With a standard 50mm lens focused at distance of 15 feet, for instance, the depth-of-field scale indicates that everything from about 8 feet to 150 feet will be sharp at a setting of f/16. At f/5.6, however, the depth of field will be reduced to from 12 feet to 20 feet. Note, too, that the shorter the

The depth-of-field and distance scales on your camera are convenient neighbors (opposite top). You can discover how much of your picture in depth will be in acceptable focus by consulting the scales. With the lens set at f/11 and focused at 15 feet, everything from just inside 10 feet to just beyond 30 feet would be reasonably sharp (opposite center). When the camera is focused at a close distance, the depth of field is very much curtailed. With the setting of f/11 but focus set at 3 feet, the depth of field extends only from about 2¾ feet through 3 1/3 feet (opposite).

Depth-of-Field Markings

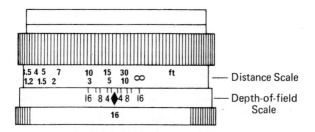

Distance Scale

Depth-of-field Scale

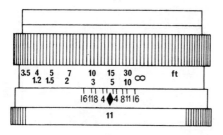

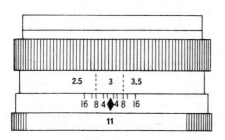

Typical Depth-of-Field Charts

55mm f/1.7

		F/Number					(in feet)
	1.7	**2.8**	**4**	**5.6**	**8**	**11**	**16**
∞	∞ 175'	∞ 107'	∞ 75'	∞ 53'	∞ 38'	∞ 27'	∞ 19'
30	36' 1" 25' 8"	41' 6" 23' 6"	49' 5" 21' 7"	67' 7" 19' 4"	141' 16'10"	∞ 14' 3"	∞ 11' 9"
10	10' 7" 9' 5-7/8"	10'12" 9' 2-1/4"	11' 5" 8'10-5/8"	12' 2" 8' 5-7/8"	13' 5" 7'11-7/8"	15' 7" 7' 4-5/8"	20' 5" 6' 8"
5	5' 1-1/2" 4'10-1/2"	5' 2-5/8" 4' 9-5/8"	5' 3-3/4" 4' 8-5/8"	5' 5-1/2" 4' 7-3/8"	5' 8-1/8" 4' 5-5/8"	6' 1/4" 4' 3-3/8"	6' 7" 4' 1/2"
3	3' 1/2" 2'11-1/2"	3' 7/8" 2'11-1/8"	3' 1-1/4" 2'10-7/8"	3' 1-3/4" 2'10-3/8"	3' 2-1/2" 2'10-3/8"	3' 3-3/4" 2' 9-3/4"	3' 5-1/2" 2' 7-3/4"
2	2' 1/8" 1'11-7/8"	2' 1/4" 1'11-3/4"	2' 1/2" 1'11-5/8"	2' 3/4" 1'11-3/8"	2' 1" 1'11-1/8"	2' 1-1/2" 1'10-3/4"	2' 2" 1'10-1/4"

(left axis: Focusing Distance)

135mm f/3.5

		F/Number						(in feet)
	2.8	**3.5**	**4**	**5.6**	**8**	**11**	**16**	**22**
∞	∞ 246'	∞ 518'	∞ 449'	∞ 318'	∞ 225'	∞ 159'	∞ 113'	∞ 80'
50	54' 1" 46' 6"	55. 2" 45' 9"	56' 1" 45' 1"	59' 1" 43' 4"	63'11" 41' 1"	72' 3" 38' 3"	88' 8" 23'11"	131' 31'
20	20' 7" 19' 5"	20' 9" 19' 4"	20'11" 19' 2"	21' 3" 18'11"	21'10" 18' 6"	22' 8" 17'11"	24' 0" 17' 2"	26' 3" 16' 2"
10	10' 2" 9'10"	10' 2" 9'10"	10' 2" 9' 9"	10' 3" 9' 8"	10' 5" 9' 7"	10' 7" 9' 5"	10'10" 9' 3"	11' 3" 9'-1/4"
5	5'-3/8" 4'11-5/8"	5'-1/2" 4'11-1/2"	5'-1/2" 4'11-1/2"	5'-5/8" 4'11-3/8"	5' 1" 4'11"	5' 1-3/4" 4'10-5/8"	5' 2-1/8" 4'10-1/8"	5' 3" 4' 9-3/8"

(left axis: Focusing Distance)

As these abbreviated depth-of-field charts show, depth of field is affected by the f/stop in use, the distance focused on, and the focal length of the lens. Consult one of the charts. You will discover that, at a certain focusing distance, the smaller the aperture (higher f/number) the greater the depth of field and the closer the distance focused on, the shallower the depth of field at a given f/number. Compare the two charts. At any distance and f/number combination, the depth of field will be shallower with the longer lens.

distance from the subject to the camera, the shallower the depth of field at any given f/stop. Likewise, the longer the focal length of your lens, the shallower the depth of field at any given distance and f/stop combination. Thus, depth of field depends on three factors: the f/stop chosen, the distance focused on, and the focal length of the lens.

When photographing nature subjects you must decide how much or little you want to fall within your depth of field. It might seem at first that "as much as possible" would be the answer. Not always. Often, in photography as in all things, less is more. In many bird or flower close-ups, only the subjects are rendered in sharp detail. In the case of the flower close-ups, the short focusing distance probably curtailed the depth of field. In bird photographs the shallow depth of field is, more often than not, due to the use of a long lens. In both cases the limited range of sharpness can well become an asset. You may elect to focus carefully on the subject, then open up the lens to maximum aperture (increasing the shutter speed to compensate for the increased exposure) to throw distracting or extraneous fore- or background elements out of focus. For landscape or grand-scale subjects, just the opposite technique might prove appropriate to maximize depth of field — stopping down to a small aperture (higher f/number) and choosing a slower shutter speed. The choice is yours.

Focus

An occasional out-of-focus shot may express your poetic soul, but in most nature photography the pedestrian point is to illustrate nature, and that means to see the subject clearly — often in greater detail than it can be seen by the naked eye. In short, sharp focus is important.

The focusing ring on your lens moves the front elements of the lens forward and backward, away from and toward the film. When the lens is entirely retracted, it is focused at infinity; when fully extended, at the closest focusing distance possible with that lens. The far-focus mark on your lens is always infinity; but the near focus will vary, depending on the focal length and design of the lens.

Perfect focus exists only in one plane, and despite the reassurance offered previously by the concept of depth of field, only objects located at the specific distance on which you focus will be rendered perfectly sharp. Everything lying in front or back of that distance will be progressively less sharp. Thus, focusing should be as exact as possible. If you're using an SLR, open up the lens to its largest aperture to admit the maximum amount of light and restrict depth of field to the minimum while focusing. That way you won't be fooled by a dim image or one that appears sharp but isn't. Once you've focused, you can stop down to whatever f/stop you please for your shot. (Modern automatic lenses open up after each shot for focusing, then stop down to the preselected f/stop when you press the shutter release.)

Nature work often requires quick, reflexive action on the part of the photographer. To prepare yourself to cope with fast-moving subjects, you should become as familiar and dexterous with your equipment as possible. No one ever wore out a camera by handling it — carefully. Practice quick focusing on objects around your home or yard. While such "dry shooting" may at first earn you nothing but looks of perplexity from your friends and neighbors, it may turn you into a photographic fast gun who will someday bag a perfect bird or animal shot.

Prefocusing

Prefocusing is a trick used by almost all professional action photographers. Animals, especially birds, will often return to the same spot time and again. Once you have located a perching place, sunning spot, or whatever, simply position yourself, focus on that point, and wait quietly for a subject to appear in your viewer. Then make your exposure without fumbling.

Similarly, you can place your area of acceptable focus within a zone by consulting the distance and depth-of-field scales on your lens. Whether a herd

Zone Focusing with Normal Lenses

For 50mm Lens Used on 35mm Camera

	Close focus	Focus at	Far Focus
Near subjects at $f/8$	4'8"	6'	8'5"
Middle distance subjects at $f/8$	6'3"	9'	15'10"
Landscapes and far subjects at $f/8$	10'6"	21'	infinity

For 75mm Lens Used on 2¼ x 2¼ Format

	Close focus	Focus at	Far Focus
Near subjects at $f/8$	6'4"	8'	10'9"
Middle distance subjects at $f/8$	9'2"	13'	22'3"
Landscapes and far subjects at $f/8$	15'6"	31'	infinity

of grazing deer or a sparkling field of flowers confronts you, decide how much of the scene you wish to render sharply. Focus on something at the far limit of your interest and something at the near limit — making mental notes of these distances. Then using the focusing scale and the depth-of-field scale on your lens barrel, choose an f/stop that will give you sufficient depth of field to take in both distances, and place the far distance at the far limit of your depth of field. If the lighting does not permit a lens opening small enough to keep everything you want in focus, trim your interest at the rear rather than at the front of the scene.. Having established a zone of focus, you can photograph with an eye to the action or composition without having to continually refocus.

Hyperfocal Distance

A last look at the lens markings will establish one final optical fact. When you focus at a given distance, that distance lies exactly 1/3 of the way into your depth of field. Thus, if you arbitrarily focus on infinity when working with distant subjects such as landscapes, you'll sacrifice 2/3 of your working depth of field, since there's nothing beyond infinity. Instead, if you place the infinity mark on your distance scale at the far limit of your working depth of field and let the point of exact focus fall where it may, you'll establish a zone of focus that encompasses everything from infinity up to the nearest distance possible with that f/stop and lens combination. The distance at which the plane of perfect focus falls when working this way is called the hyperfocal distance. By choosing the smallest-aperture/slowest-time combination practical, and focusing on the hyperfocal distance rather than infinity, you'll maximize the zone of focus and improve the overall clarity of your general shots.

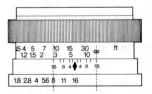

This drawing shows the correct alignment of distance and aperture scales to set the hyperfocal distance for an aperture of f/16.

Landscapes

Landscapes are among the most popular nature subjects; at the same time they are the pictures that most often fail to live up to the photographer's expectations if he allows himself to be enraptured by the gestalt, a blend of stimulus and response, most of which is invisible. The freshness or bite of the air, the song of a bird, or the sweet scents of flowers or woods — the very qualities that often move the photographer to record a scene — will not show up on his film. Instead, a strictly visual vocabulary — the scale of elements in the scene, the available light, the colors or gray tones — must be consciously used to translate the three-dimensional, grand-scale outdoors into an interesting two-dimensional, reduced-scale photograph.

Lenses for Landscapes

Your choice of lens will determine the fundamental effect of your landscape photographs. A wide-angle lens will allow you to take in a greater expanse at closer distance than you'll be able to include with a normal or a long lens. But remember the relationship of focal length to subject size: the wide-angle will cover more territory, but everything in it will be smaller. So, unless the vast expanse of land, sea, or sky is the point of your picture, or there is some interesting foreground subject such as a rock or tree to provide a point of interest, wide-angle photos risk apparent emptiness with puny mid-ground and background details. A normal lens presumably "sees" the same area as human vision with the eye's sense of scale and perspective. A long lens will allow you to isolate some distant detail in the full frame.

"Distortion"

Both long and short lenses — especially toward the extreme focal lengths — are often accused of causing "distortion." It is a bum rap. Unless there is something wrong with your lens, it does not distort; it merely performs as it was designed to perform. The result may be an image that seems incorrect or even grotesque to the human eye, which is designed to entirely different specifications.

Foreground objects in wide-angle pictures may appear to warp unnaturally forward. The larger and closer they are, the more they seem to loom — and correctly so. At close distances, even slight differences in camera-to-subject distance are emphasized. If that first boulder is only 3 feet away from the lens and the second is 6 feet away, the camera-to-subject distance is doubled from the first to the second, and their relative sizes on film will vary with the distance. If the same subjects were photographed from 30 feet away with a telephoto lens long enough to reproduce the near boulder in the same image size as with the wide-angle, the 3-foot distance between the first and second rocks would be only 1/10th the total camera-to-subject distance, and the apparent discrepancy in their sizes would be minimized. Thus, lens performance should not be referred to as distortion. The example above is one of perspective, and perspective is simply a matter of subject-to-camera distance.

Perspective effects must be considered in choosing a lens. If you choose a wide-angle in order to take in an entire tree from close up, the lens' angle of view will take in the tree from bottom to top if you tilt the camera a bit. But because the upper tree is so much farther from the camera than the base and lower branches, it will appear progressively diminished in the picture — perspective will make it seem to topple over backward. Photographed from a distance with a normal or long lens, with the film plane parallel to the subject plane, and the camera-to-tree-base and camera-to-tree-top distances in closer relation, the tree will stand upright again.

While wide-angle lenses seem to exaggerate apparent perspective, telephotos seem to compress it. Again, the supposed shortcoming of the lens is nothing more than the law of perspective governed by camera-to-subject distance. Working from a long camera-to-subject distance has the opposite effect from shooting at close range. The interval between subjects — or even the distance from the front side of a subject to its back — is less significant and less emphasized. The camera lens contradicts what the mind knows to be true. A row of telegraph poles or fenceposts running alongside an open road will seem to clump up the farther away they are; the roundness of a distant boulder will appear less emphatic at a distance than at close range. The mind knows that no one plants telephone poles or fenceposts widely spaced here and closely spaced there, and that boulders bulge whether near or far, and so it corrects the eye's vision. The camera does not. It merely sees as it sees. Thus, distant mountains are rendered as flat, overlapping layers rather than the voluptuous, well-separated masses that the eye persuades us are put out there.

The important thing is not to bemoan a lens' "distortions," but, instead, to familiarize yourself with the particular vision of each lens in order to utilize it to best advantage.

Lighting for Landscapes

Light might seem to be the element of least concern to the landscape photographer because there's not much he can do about it. Still, the

The Direction of Light

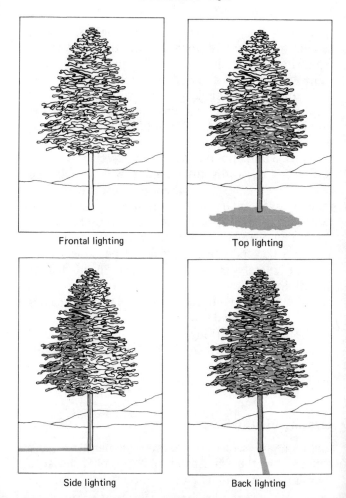

Frontal lighting

Top lighting

Side lighting

Back lighting

quality, color, and direction of the light in a landscape are the controlling factors in its mood, drama, and uniqueness.

The color of daylight changes constantly from dawn through dusk. The color balance shifts from pink at dawn, to "white" at noon, to the red of sunset, and finally to lavender after sundown. While the sun is in view, the color of its light depends on how much atmosphere it passes through before reaching you and your subject. After sundown the light appears lavender because it is the red light of the sun below the horizon being reflected by the blue sky. While we might stubbornly refer to sunlight as "white" morning, noon, or night, the specific color characteristics of the light striking your subject will affect the

The Direction of Light

As the drawings opposite show, the position of the sun will have a great effect on the picture. If you position yourself so that the sun is behind you and strikes the subject directly (front lighting), the subject will be evenly illuminated but lack shape. If the sun comes from the side of the subject (side lighting), the subject will be darker on the less-illuminated side and its shape will be more apparent. The subject will also cast a shadow. When the sun is directly over the subject (top lighting), the shadows will be harsh and will fall on the underside of the subject. If the camera is aimed directly into the light so that the subject is lit from behind (back lighting), the subject will appear as a silhouette, unless deliberate exposure adjustments are made, and the shadow will fall toward the photographer.

rendition of colors in your photograph. You can cancel out the color shift in your picture by so-called "corrective" filtration, but you'll be eliminating the sense of a specific time and place in the bargain.

On a rainy or foggy day the atmosphere is loaded with particles of water. These scatter the blue light and absorb the red, lending your pictures an overall blue cast. Filtering will do little to correct this, as blue light predominates. But again, to filter would be to destroy the sense of weather. Remember, too, that the earth's atmosphere always contains moisture, and the more distance — and atmosphere — you place between you and your subjects, the more bluishness in your picture will increase. Even the backgrounds in your normal-lens shots will go gradually blue. This phenomenon is known as aerial perspective, and for centuries it has been a way for artists to suggest distance. It serves the same function in your photographs. You'll find this blue cast in all scenic shots made with a long lens, and, if you object to it, there is no way to beat it short of decreasing the distance between you and your subject. Don't be misled by the image enlargement provided by a long lens. To decrease aerial haze and assure optimum image quality, you must approach your subject more closely.

Filters for Landscapes

For use with black-and-white film

yellow	Absorbs ultraviolet and blue violet rays.	Darkens blue skies. Emphasizes clouds. Lightens foliage and grass. Maintains good tonality in sand and snow.
dark yellow	Absorbs ultraviolet, violet and most blue rays.	Darkens water and skies. Emphasizes clouds. Increases contrast in sand and snow. Lightens yellow and red flowers.
red	Absorbs ultraviolet, blue-violet and blue and green rays.	Lightens red and yellow flowers. Darkens blue water and sky. Cuts haze and increases contrast in general.
dark red	Absorbs ultraviolet, blue-violet, green and yellow-green rays.	Darkens sky and water to almost black. Dramatizes clouds.
green	Absorbs ultraviolet, violet, blue and red rays.	Lightens foliage. Darkens sky.
blue	Absorbs red, yellow, green and ultraviolet rays.	Lightens blue water and sky. Enhances fog and haze effects.

Light balancing filters for use with color films

yellowish	Lowers color temperature of natural light.	Produces warmer colors when light is bluish as on overcast day when subject is in shadow.
bluish	Raises the color temperature of natural light.	Produces cooler colors when light is too red as it is at sunset.

Other filters for landscapes

neutral density	Stops some of all wavelengths of light. Does not affect color. Used with both b/w and color films.	Used to reduce exposure when photographing in bright sunlight with high-speed film.
polarizing	Eliminates reflections and glare.	Useful in shooting marine scenes. Darkens sky and lightens clouds when sun is not directly overhead.
ultraviolet	Stops ultraviolet rays.	Penetrates haze. Used to sharpen results on overcast days or when using long lens.
skylight	Reduces excess blue.	Used to warm up results when shooting on overcast days or when subject is in shadow.

The two photographs shown on these pages demonstrate the practical effect of using filters for landscape photography. Photographer Robert Walch photographed the scene first without using a filter (left). Then he added a red filter, made the necessary exposure adjustment, and photographed the scene again (right). The filter's

effect is especially evident in the separation of the clouds and blue sky.

The photograph on the following pages again demonstrates the dramatic potential of filters for landscape work.

Photo by Robert Walch.

Composing Your Landscape

If Mohammed couldn't move mountains, how can a landscape photographer hope to compose his shots? The subject is immovable but, fortunately, the photographer is not. While there are no sure rules for successful composition, any photographer – and especially the novice – must continually view and study his scene in the hope of achieving a strong visual arrangement. In composing your shot, seek out strong shapes and elements, interesting shadows, or a variety of textures – those details that make the scene interesting on-the-spot and can make your photograph an interesting object worthy of a long look, not something that can be taken in at a glance.

A Sense of Depth

You can establish a sense of depth in your photograph by deliberately including some foreground element to provide framing. A tree trunk at one side of your shot or a branch running across the top will maintain the idea of near and far and may make it more interesting than one of those pictures in which everything is way over there. Framing periodically falls into severe disrepute, and small wonder when some books suggest dragging along plastic branches to stick into the view. But, used appropriately, and with natural elements, it will maintain a feeling of depth near and far, and by establishing a point of view will suggest your presence in the final shot.

Focus

A generous area of "in-focus" detail will enhance the overall interest and readability of your landscape photographs. By using the hyperfocal-distance setting discussed earlier on in the chapter on *The Camera's Controls* you can maximize the depth of field for your lens and f/stop. Occasionally, you may want to take just the opposite tack, and focus selectively on one plane or element in your view. If you are using a wide-angle lens, selective focus is difficult because of the lens' generous depth of field. But a very wide aperture, combined with a short focusing distance, will emphasize that single, sharp detail. Long lenses have shallow depth of field as an optical characteristic. Thus, they are useful in isolating mid-range or distant details. But remember, the longer your lens and the shallower the depth of field, the more critical the need to focus exactly.

Metering and Exposure

The metering and exposure techniques for landscape photography are perhaps the most complicated and bedeviling part of the subject. A studio photographer working with a couple of lights or a strobe set up may look like Merlin the Magician. But, he controls his lights, and what he's doing is child's play compared with the considerations and trial and error of successful landscape work. Much of available-light outdoor photography can only be considered and mastered by you, on the spot. The following can only be a summary of the points you should consider before taking your picture.

Tonal Range

Tonal range refers to the extremes of contrast — from the lightest to the darkest shades — in the picture. A scene viewed on a bright, sunny day will feature rich, dark shadows and bright highlights. On an overcast day the same scene will have a shorter range of contrast from the lightest through the darkest tones. If you wish to capture the detail in both the lightest and darkest areas of your scene, you must choose a film capable of recording the range of tones present. Black-and-white films have much greater tonal range than do color films.

Selective Exposure

Landscape photography offers the photographer both exposure problems and possibilities. For a particular scene, more than one exposure combination may prove correct — depending on the intent of the photograph and those aspects of the scene which the photographer wishes to emphasize. In the illustration opposite the general reading given by a built-in meter was followed. Because of the bright backlighting, the framing tree and branches become silhouettes and the shadows go black. Photo by Rafael Fraguada.

In a black-and-white exposure, an area can be three to four stops under- or overexposed and still capture some detail. In color, a two stop difference more or less will produce burned-out highlights or black shadows. You can limit the tonal range of the subject somewhat by eliminating an overly bright sky or a deeply shadowed area from the composition. A good rule of thumb is to expose for the shadows in black-and-white work, and for the highlights in color.

If you own a spot meter, you can single out a small interesting section from which to take your reading. If not, your meter, especially the built-in type, may be thrown off by some overly bright or dark area of your overall view.

Approach the part of the scene you wish to expose for, or find a sample of similar brightness close at hand, and make your reading from that.

Taking Your Reading

Take your meter meading from whatever part of the scene you wish to emphasize. If the texture of that tree bark, the leaves and twigs littering the forest floor, or those rocks in the foreground are most important to you, take a reading from them and set your camera accordingly. Don't expect, however, that everything else will show up in your picture. Your films can only deal with one light level at a time. If you meter and expose for detail rendition in dark areas, the highlight areas will be overexposed and appear overly bright and lacking detail in your picture. Such is photography. You must choose your emphasis.

Shutter-Speed Choice

Shutter speed may seem inconsequential in photographing a nice static landscape. However, it must be considered in both its functions: as a complement to your aperture for correct exposure and as an action stopper.

A slow shutter speed will allow you to use a small aperture and thereby gain maximum depth of field in your landscape photo. Despite the seeming calm of even the most peaceful scene, grasses and branches sway, leaves flutter, and streams flow on by. If you wish to stop the action, you must choose an appropriate shutter speed. Remember that motion blur is related to distance. Thus the leaves on a middle-ground or distant tree can be stopped at 1/50th second or 1/100th second, while those swaying foreground reeds or grasses may require 1/250th second of 1/500th second to freeze them. Remember, too, that scenics need not seem entirely frozen. The blur of a flowing stream or cascading waterfall, or the twinkle of the blowing leaves on a static tree, may be the very element that attracted you to your subject.

Special Landscape Subjects

Different sorts of scenes and weather conditions will confront you with a variety of working considerations. A general listing of basic landscape subjects and conditions and some basic techniques follows.

A Normal Scene

One man's normal is another man's predicament. Consider taking a straightforward photograph of a general scene on a bright, windless day. A standard exposure, $f/16$ at the shutter-speed setting closest to the ASA rating of your film — for example, 1/125th second for Plus-X, which has an ASA of 125 — will produce a nice, average exposure. If you stand the way Kodak tells you to, with the sun behind you, your subjects will cast their shadows behind them, eliminating many contrast considerations. You make your exposure and are treated to a well-exposed, evenly illuminated, flat-as-a-pancake result. If that's what you wanted, fine. But if it was the angling shadows, or the textures emphasized by cross-lighting, or even the dramatic silhouette of a back-lit subject that attracted you, or if you can't wait for the sun to obey the instruction book, you must solve your problem on the spot.

If you're after those deep, rich shadows, let them go thoroughly underexposed to emphasize them as dark shapes and patterns without detail or texture, and expose instead for the highlighted areas. If it is the texture in the grass or leaves or on the dark rock that caught your eye, make sure that you emphasize that area or element in focusing and exposure. And if you must point your camera into the sun, "backlighting" the subject, try to keep the sun above your frame, and expose for the dark, near side if you wish detail and don't mind a burned-out sky. Conversely, expose for the background sky if you wish silhouettes. If you do include the sun, beware of flare, which will produce burned-out edges on your subject, or ghosts, or those bright spots that may mar, or make, your picture. Ghosts are produced by the bright light bouncing around inside your lens. If you center the sun in your viewer and choose a small aperture, you may succeed in getting a star-shaped sun without ghosts. Place it up in one corner and you'll get a repeated light spot running diagonally down and across your picture — blip, blip, blip.

A sun shade is an inexpensive necessity in shooting across or into the sun. It acts simply to block stray light from entering your lens from the side or above. You should have one for every lens. Each should be of sufficient width and depth for the lens on which it is to be used. A shallow, wide shade, designed for use on a wide-angle lens, will do little to keep stray light from entering your

telephoto. And a deep, narrow shade for a telephoto will block the wide view of your wide-angle
lens and chop off the corners of your pictures. The
lens shade also serves as a handy lens umbrella on
rainy days and will generally protect your lens
from scratches, mars, and airborne grit and sand.

Beach Scenes, Deserts, and Snowcapes

Cameras and film are as subject to sun or snow
blindness as the eye. And, beaches, deserts, and
snowscapes have brightness in common. Not only
does light come from above, but it is bounced back
from the light ground. If you fall into the habit of
using fast films as your standard working stock,
you will be entirely unprepared for wide-aperture,
slow-shutter work in overly bright situations. In
bright light, a high ASA film will limit your
exposures to fast-shutter, small-aperture combinations when just the opposite may strike your
fancy. So whether you head for the Sahara or the
polar ice cap in summer, take along some nice, slow,
and medium-speed film to expand your range, plus a
selection of neutral-density filters (see the chapter
on *Films and Filters*) to cut down light without
disturbing the color or tonal balance of your
photograph. You can beat the overexposure risks
by making your sand or snow exposures either
early or late in the day. Not only will light be less,
but its raking angle will emphasize the surface

texture and shadow patterns of the landscape.

Photographing near water introduces an invisible but influential element into your picture taking: ultraviolet light. The moisture in the air leads to a scattering of the blue and ultraviolet rays in the sunlight and in light from the sky. Those same unseen rays that tan your skin also affect your film. Overexposure in black-and-white, or a blue cast in color, may well result. A UV filter will minimize the problem.

Snowscapes may also suffer from overexposure and unexpected color casts. Remember, in taking your reading, that the major portion of your scene is white and meters frequently fail when directed toward very bright light. If you wish other elements in your shot to be other than grossly underexposed, you must make selective meter readings — a good spot meter is invaluable under such circumstances. The time of day will affect the color rendition of your white snow by affecting the color of the light striking it. Snowscapes prove, often to the beginner's surprise, that shadows are blue. All these color effects in snowscapes can be undone by the use of light-balancing filters, if you wish. (See the chapter on *Films and Filters.*)

Pictures by Moonlight

Moonlight has an eternal and understandable charm for lovers; but it is a pain in the exposure meter for photographers. Exposure problems are just the opposite from those mentioned above: there is less light than you think, not more. Your eye will become accustomed to the low light on a seemingly brightly lit moonlit night. But the moon does not produce light; it merely reflects some of the sunlight falling on it. For all its romantic appeal, the moon is a second-hand light source — despite its seeming brilliance against the dark night sky and shadows, moonlight is only about 1/6000th as intense as sunlight.

A tripod is a prime necessity for night photography because time exposures are the rule, not the exception. A small pocket flashlight will help you read the dials and settings on your camera. And, for safety's sake, make a variety of exposures. Film responds in a very uncertain way with time-exposures and low light. Don't jeopardize your results by saving time or film by making only an exposure or two.

The moon may be an important element in your composition, but don't be the victim of your eye. The eye may see the moon as larger and more important than it will come out in your photograph. The phenomenon is called the moon illusion, and it makes the moon seem larger when it is viewed in relation to some earthbound element. The moon, in truth, remains equally distant from the earth, and the same size, from rise to set.

Although a hazy night may diffuse and enlarge it slightly, if you wish to enlarge and emphasize it in your picture, you must rely on photographic means. Throwing the moon out of focus and focusing instead on some nearby tree or landscape feature will enlarge it somewhat, but those dramatic saucer-sized moons looming over the landscape are purely the products of long lenses.

The combination of a full, bright moon, a clear night, and a photogenic landscape does not occur as often as photographers hope. You can beat the game somewhat by seizing two of the ingredients when they do occur and holding them in store for the final touch. On a bright, full-moonlit night expose a roll of film of the moon and sky, setting the exposure or filtering to get full details in the moon. Keep the moon in the same place in each frame and remember where it is — make a sketch if necessary. A mid-range telephoto lens will give a good sized moon. A 300mm lens or longer will make the moon loom surreally large. Then rewind the film, being sure to leave the leader out of the cassette, and wait for the perfect landscape.

A scratch on the film leader, made when you load the film for the first series of exposures, aligned with a small piece of tape on the camera interior will enable you to reload the same film in perfect alignment to superimpose the landscape over the latent moon image, resulting in a "moon over Miami" or anywhere you want it. A normal or wide-angle lens for the second shooting, combined with a telephoto for the first, will create the illusion of a vast landscape sleeping under a huge moon. The landscape exposures can even be made in broad daylight, underexposed or heavily filtered to create the illusion of evening or night.

Sunrises and Sunsets

Photographing sunrises and sunsets necessitates that you aim your camera directly into the sun. Because the light is traveling through so much atmosphere, it is diffused before reaching your lens, so you need not worry about flare or ghosts. The diffusion will make the sun seem enlarged. But, as with moonscapes, using a long lens will produce a more dramatic photograph. Expose for the sun and sky or you'll simply get a burned-in, shapeless glare.

Aerials

If you don't have the fare for a private plane and a pilot, a window seat in a commercial plane will afford you the opportunity to take aerial photographs. Many commercial flights announce your passage over well-known geographical features. You can also record beautiful high-level cloud formations and sun and moon effects from your aerial vantage point. Choose a location away from the wing to have a clear view. Position your camera as close as possible to the glass to avoid any reflections from the inside surface and drape your coat or a blanket over your head to eliminate stray light from within the plane. Remember, there is bound to be a good deal of atmosphere between you and your subject, so use your UV filter or warming filter to keep your pictures from having a blue cast. And never lean your camera against the window or window frame for stability, the vibration of the plane will ruin your exposure.

Special Cameras and Equipment for Landscapes

The View Camera

The view camera remains the workhorse of professional landscape photographers. The ability to adjust the positions of the lens and film plane in relation to the subject allows subjects to be rendered square on, even when no square-on vantage point exists.

The "Perspective Control" Lens

Nikon, manufacturers of one of the most popular 35mm cameras, has introduced a "PC" (perspective control) lens, which allows for some perspective correction. The front element of the lens and its optical center can be shifted off center to allow for visually correct rendition of tall objects seen at close quarters. But the "PC" lens on the 35mm format is only one small step toward the flexibility of the view camera system.

The Superwides

Those superwide views that span the horizon, sometimes all 360 degrees of it, can be produced in a variety of ways. Super-wide-angle lenses mounted on special 35mm cameras, such as the Hologon Ultrawide by Zeiss, offer a 100-degree angle of view without a hint of distortion or change in perspective compacted into the space of a normal 35mm frame. The Panon Widelux offers a lens that actually swings in an arc to cover 140 degrees of the scene. The film in the camera is held in a similar arc to avoid distortion or loss of focus at the edges of the frame. The Widelux records its view on a wider than normal frame — each exposure measures 2 1/3" across, nearly an inch more than the standard 35mm frame.

Views of 360 degrees, as if you stood in one spot and scanned the horizon from one point all the way around to that point again, are made in just that way. A super-wide-angle camera can produce such a set of panoramic shots in fewer views, but you can do the same thing with your normal lens and equipment. Mount the camera on a tripod and level it carefully with a spirit level.

Simply make a series of exposures, rotating the camera between each, and being sure to keep the horizon steady between them. Allow a small overlap rather than risking missing a section. You can splice the frames together yourself in printing or have a custom printer do it for you. Such a series is well worth whatever time, trouble, or money you spend in producing it; it will remain the ultimate evidence of your having been there, on the spot, when things were just so.

Close-ups

Even your first close-up photographs will prove the personal possibilities of nature photography. No marked trails will lead you to, or any scenic lookouts afford you, the beautiful array and variety of nature seen at close hand. The splendid perfection of these minute designs may even impart some wisdom as to the true balance of things.

The camera can show a world unknown to the unaided eye. The eye can focus down to a near limit of about eight inches while the camera can be made to focus on subjects only fractions of an inch away. The new perspective can be gained only by perception coupled with consideration of the new photographic possibilities and problems introduced by working at close range. The intention and perception necessarily must be left to you – the possibilities and problems will be the subject of this chapter.

The Practical Problems

The smaller citizens of life's community – plants, flowers, insects – are among the most frequent subjects for close-up shooting. They provide an infinite variety of subjects for the photographer who has the patience and the desire to seek them out.

Flowers will bloom, and go to seed, and insects will live out their lives from birth, through mating, to death, in blissful ignorance of you and your camera. It falls to you to discover them and to adjust your schedule to theirs. Familiarity, in photography, never breeds contempt — it breeds good pictures. A collection of illustrated nature guides is a worthwhile investment. The series by Roger Tory Peterson, including volumes on flowers, insects, trees, and so forth, is especially useful, and widely available.

The principal problem in photographing living subjects at close range is simply that they move. An almost imperceptible movement can be magnified in close-ups, rendering a picture taken at too slow a shutter speed a hopeless blur. Flowers will sway even in the slightest breeze. If you watch the pattern of their motion carefully, you may discern an instant in which they seem to pause. That's the instant to make your exposure at the fastest possible shutter speed. A 1/500th second will arrest the dance of the flowers under most circumstances.

A simple windbreak will prove a valuable addition to your equipment if you plan to photograph plants and flowers close up. A sheet of heavy, white cardboard, or a shield of plastic or white fabric, carefully placed out of the camera's view, will reduce movement to a minimum. As with all field equipment, portability should be a consideration in your choice of a windbreak. Although white cardboard is inexpensive and widely available, its rigidity makes it cumbersome. Fabric or plastic, on the other hand, can be folded and stowed in a camera bag or pocket, or even wrapped around the legs of a tripod, for easy carrying.

Like flowers, insects also have the frustrating habit of moving about — usually just after you have focused on them. Some books suggest keeping your insect subjects in an ice chest or freezer before photographing them, or blasting them with carbon dioxide to cool them down and thereby reduce their motion. But a distinguished entomologist-photographer cautions that to the expert eye pictures of frozen insects are as obvious as pictures of drunken humans. Instead, for a particularly handsome photo of a spider, he chased the poor thing until it was tired out and slowed down sufficiently for him to photograph. If you find that neither freezing nor stalking appeals to you, your best bet is to photograph insects early in the morning, when they are less active. Still another possibility is to prepare your working set up, prefocus on a small rock or twig, and then at the last moment remove it and substitute your insect subject.

Flying insects are even more difficult to corner and control. You'd best discover or rig up something that attracts them, prefocus, and wait. One successful butterfly photographer goes to exhaustive lengths. He sets up, prefocuses on a likely flower, and then covers all the nearby flowers with paper sacks so nothing competes for the attention of a passing subject.

Choosing a static subject will, of course, eliminate the problem of subject motion from your close-up work and leave you free to explore for an interesting abstract pattern, texture, or purely photographic subject. The pattern of a tree's bark or the surface of a rock can lend variety and a sense of scale to your landscape coverage. The environment of a shallow tidal pool, its surface glare penetrated by a polarizing filter, can demonstrate the complexity of nature. Even the least noticeable subject, seen in detail previously unperceived by the human eye, can achieve beauty and interest through the intervention of the camera.

Another simple but bedeviling problem of close-up subjects is that so many are located at ground level. You can always aim down at them, but a worm's-eye view somehow seems more appropriate and natural. Bring along a yard or so of some waterproof material to kneel on, and you will be able to get down to your subjects' level dry-kneed and unmuddied. Properly prone, you will probably discover that the design of your camera's viewer makes it extremely clumsy to use in this position.

A fine time to find out! If you are shooting with a 2¼" x 2¼" reflex, with its ground-glass viewer on top, you are set. But the finders on 35mm SLRs and rangefinder cameras simply become useless when the camera is placed at ground level. Some SLRs allow for (by removal of the prism finder) viewing in the ground glass. Such viewing is often made difficult by light from above or from the side illuminating the top of the ground glass. An accessory waist-level viewer includes the ground glass and surrounding pop-up shadow box to assure a clear, bright image. Or, a special 45-degree or 90-degree viewer may be available for your camera to angle the image up to your eye for easier, more accessible low-level viewing.

The Photographic Problems

Camera movement can mar your close-ups just as much as subject motion can. A good, sturdy tripod is helpful. Some of the more elaborate (and more expensive) tripods feature a reversible center post, which can be removed, reversed, and reinserted with the camera mount extended down between the legs. (This is a boon in photographing ground-level, close-up subjects.) A short-legged, table-top tripod is a good alternate support, and is much lighter and more compact to carry into the field than a full-sized tripod.

The firmest support is rendered useless if your camera is jolted during the exposure. If you are using an SLR, lock the mirror up before releasing your shutter. (This two-step exposure sequence is possible with many models. Check your owner's manual for instructions for your particular camera.) Also, use a cable release to trigger the exposure smoothly.

The second photographic problem with close-ups is simply getting close enough to fill the frame with a tiny subject. Theoretically, no lens can focus closer than the distance equal to its focal length. In practice, near-focus limits are somewhat longer than theory allows. Normal lenses will focus down to about 2 or 3 feet; wide-angle lenses, somewhat less, telephotos, somewhat more. For close-up work, the enlarged image size of the longer focal-length lenses is counteracted by the increased minimum camera-to-subject distance. To achieve frame-filling close-ups, with the subject recorded life-sized or thereabouts on the film, additional optical equipment becomes necessary, along with special framing and exposure adjustments.

Remember from the chapter on *The Camera's Controls* that the closer the distance focused on, the shallower the depth of field. At very close distances the depth of field is reduced to less than an inch. Thus, focusing must be precise not only on the subject, but usually on some detail or section of the subject. Remember, too, that exact focus lies in a plane and that even the slightest subject or camera movement forward or backward can be ruinous. Inaccuracy in focus is unmistakeable. But the limited depth of field can be used creatively to isolate some aspect of your subject for emphasis.

Close-up Lenses and Attachments

Focusing on closer than normal camera-to-subject distances can be achieved by three means: supplementary lenses, which are mounted in front of your lens; extension tubes or bellows, inserted behind your lens; or special macro lenses, designed for close-up work.

Close-up Devices

Three close-up devices are illustrated opposite. The first, a close-up or supplementary lens, is mounted in front of the camera lens and can be used on fixed-lens and rangefinder cameras as well as on the interchangeable-lens SLR. The second and third devices are inserted between the lens and camera body and thus can only be used on interchangeable-lens cameras. Tubes and bellows are generally used only on SLR's because of the framing and focusing difficulties that would be introduced if they were used with other models. A special reflex viewing device is available to adapt some rangefinder cameras for use with tubes and bellows.

Close-up Devices

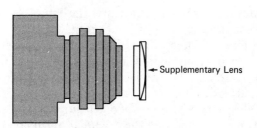

← Supplementary Lens

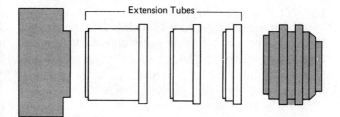

Extension Tubes

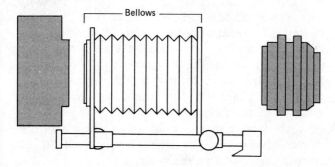

Bellows

Supplementary (Close-up) Lenses

Supplementary (close-up) lenses are the simplest and least expensive solution. Fitted on the front of your lens like a filter, they alter entirely the focusing range of your lens. Close-up lenses from different manufacturers are labeled with various and unrelated codes, but their strength is uniformly rated in diopters. When you add a 1-diopter lens to your prime lens and set the focus at infinity, you'll find that a subject 1 meter (39 inches) from the lens is in focus, no matter what the actual focal length or usual minimum focusing distance of the lens may be. A 2-diopter supplementary lens focuses at ½ meter (19½ inches) with the prime lens focused at infinity, a 3-diopter at 1/3 meter (13 inches), and so on; simply divide the diopter strength into 39 inches to get the new focusing distance at infinity setting. When you focus your lens on a distance closer than infinity, the close-up lens allows you to focus even nearer than the above distances. The accompanying chart indicates the effects of close-up lens used on your normal lens (50mm on most 35mm cameras). With longer focal-length lenses, the focusing distances will remain the same but the magnifications will be greater and the field of view correspondingly smaller; with shorter than normal lenses, the magnification will be smaller, the field of view larger, but the focusing again will be the same.

Close-up lenses can be used on any camera — even one without interchangeable lenses. With SLR cameras, the supplementary lens' effect on image size, as well as correct framing and focusing, can all be seen in the viewer. For twin-lens reflexes, close-up lenses are often sold in pairs to allow for focusing then exposure, without having to transfer the lens from the focusing to the taking lens. There is still a discrepancy in framing when the TLR's two lenses view the subject so closely. This close-up parallax can be corrected by mounting the camera on a tripod, framing and focusing through the viewing lens, then jacking the camera up exactly the distance between the two lenses so that the taking lens is brought into the position of the viewing lens for the exposure. Special jacks are sold to raise the camera just so, but you can do the same thing, without an unnecessary outlay of cash and the addition of an unnecessary piece of equipment, by merely measuring the distance from the center of one lens to the center of the other, marking this distance on the post of your tripod and remembering to raise your camera before you take your picture. Even the simplest, least expensive cameras can be used with supplementary lenses and corrected for parallax by using an improvised cardboard or wood-and-wire framing and measuring device such as that illustrated in the drawing on page 158.

Choosing a Supplementary Lens

	Focal Length	Use on Lens no Longer Than
+1=	1,000-mm	500-mm
+2=	500-mm	250-mm
+3=	334-mm	180-mm
+4=	250-mm	125-mm
+5=	200-mm	100-mm
+6=	166-mm	85-mm
+7=	142-mm	75-mm
+8=	125-mm	65-mm
+10=	100-mm	50-mm

(left axis label: Supplementary Diopter Strength)

Supplementary lenses are the simplest close-up attachments. For optimum results, the diopter strength of the supplementary lens should not exceed certain limits when used with prime lenses of certain focal lengths. The recommended prime-lens focal lengths and supplementary diopter strengths are given in the chart.

Close-up Magnifications (Reproduction Ratios)

	Focal Length	50-mm	55-mm	85-mm	100-mm	135-mm	200-mm
+1	1,000-mm	1:20	1:18	1:12	1:10	1:7.5	1:5
+2	500-mm	1:10	1:9	1:6	1:5	1:3.7	1:2.5
+3	333-mm	1:6.6	1:6	1:4	1:3.3	1:2.5	1:1.7
+4	250-mm	1:5	1:4.5	1:3	1:2.5	1:1.9	—
+5	200-mm	1:4	1:4	1:2.4	1:2	—	—
+6	167-mm	1:3.4	1:3	—	—	—	—
+8	125-mm	1:2.5	1:2.3	—	Not Recommended	—	—
+10	100-mm	1:2	1:2	—	—	—	—

(left axis label: Supplementary Lenses)

The chart above indicates the ratios between subject size and film-image size which occur when various supplementary lenses are used in combination with different prime lenses focused at infinity. A 50 mm lens, for example, with a 1 diopter supplementary attached, will produce a film-image size that is 1/20th — or 5 percent — the size of the subject.

Subject-Distance and Area-of-Coverage Chart for Supplementary Lenses

Close-up Lens	Focused Distance	Subject Distance (inches)	Area covered 50mm lens on 35mm camera	Area covered 75mm Lens on 2¼x2¼" camera
+1	infinity	39"	19x28"	30x30"
	20	33-3/4"	16x24"	25-1/2x25-1/2"
	10	29-5/8"	14x21"	22x22"
	5	23-3/4"	11x16-5/8"	17-1/8x17-1/8"
	3½ feet	20-3/8"	10-1/4x15-1/2"	14-3/8x14-3/8"
+2	infinity	19-1/2"	9-3/8x14"	14-3/4x14-3/4"
	20	18"	8-5/8x12-7/8"	13-1/2x13-1/2"
	10	16-7/8"	8-1/2x12-7/8"	12-1/2x12-1/2"
	5	14-7/8"	6-7/8x10-3/8"	10-3/4x10-3/4"
	3½ feet	13-3/8"	6-1/8x 9-1/4"	8-7/8x8-7/8"
+3	infinity	13"	6-1/4x9-3/8"	9-7/8x9-7/8"
	20	12-3/8"	5-7/8x8-7/8"	9-1/4x9-1/4"
	10	11-7/8"	5-5/8x8-3/8"	8-3/4x8-3/4"
	5	10-3/4"	4-7/8x7-1/2"	7-3/4x7-3/4"
	3½ feet	10"	4-1/2x6-7/8"	7x7"
+4 (3+1)	infinity	9-7/8"	4-5/8x6-5/8"	7-3/8x7-3/8"
	20	9-1/2"	4-1/2x6-5/8"	7x7"
	3½ feet	8"	3-5/8x5-3/8"	5-1/2x5-1/2"
+5 (3+2)	infinity	7-7/8"	3-3/4x5-5/8"	5-7/8x5-7/8"
	20	7-5/8"	3-1/2x5-3/8"	5-5/8x5-5/8"
	3½ feet	6-1/2"	3x4-3/8"	4-1/2x4-1/2"

When using supplementary lenses the subject distance should actually be measured to assure exact focus and compute image magnification. The distance from the subject to the front surface of the supplementary lens is the subject distance.

A Close-up Distance- and Field-Finder

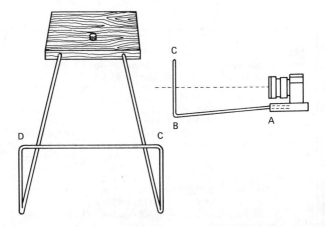

An easily constructed wire frame can adapt the rangefinder camera for use with supplementary lenses without parallax error. More than one frame, constructed following the measurements given in the accompanying table, will make it possible to use supplementaries of different diopter strengths.

Close-up Lens	ab	for 50mm lens		for 45mm lens	
		bc	cd	bc	cd
+1	39	18½	28	20½	31
+2	19½	9½	14	10½	15
+3	13	6	9	6¾	10
+4	9½	4½	7	5	7½
+5	8	3¾	5	4	6
+6	6½	3¼	4¾	3½	5

*measurements are for use with camera lens set on infinity

Extension Tubes or Bellows

Extension tubes or bellows enlarge the subject by moving the lens farther from the film. Ordinarily, when you focus your lens on subjects closer than infinity, the front section of the lens extends. The amount of movement built into your lens sets its near focusing distance. When you insert a light-tight tube or bellows behind the lens, the distance for the rear element of the lens to the film is increased. The image size is increased proportionately, just as it would be if you increased the distance between a projector and the screen.

The use of tubes and bellows is restricted to cameras with through-the-lens viewing: SLR s and view cameras. On other types of cameras the complications introduced in framing and exposure calculations would undo the convenience and utility of tubes and bellows.

Tubes are rigid metal rings that usually come in sets of two or three in different lengths. Bellows are light-tight, accordion-pleated attachments mounted on a rigid metal track. The bellows allow more flexibility because they can be expanded or contracted to the exact extension desired. With tubes you must remove the lens and add or subtract sections in order to change extension.

The amount of extension establishes the degree of image magnification. The image size is referred to as magnification even when the ratio is less than

1:1. Smaller than life-sized images are expressed as decimals: ½ life-sized would be a .5 magnification. You can compute the magnification for any extension, or calculate how much extension is necessary to achieve a desired magnification, by using a simple formula. Extension= (Magnification+ 1) x (Focal length of the lens) − (Focal length of the lens).

For example, with a 50mm lens and a desired magnification of 1 x (life-sized):

$$E = (1 + 1) \times (50) - (50)$$
$$E = (2 \times 50) - (50)$$
$$E = 50$$

Thus, you would need an extension of 50mm.

Conversely, you can determine the degree of magnification with a certain extension and a certain lens. For example, with a 75mm extension on a 50mm lens:

$$75 = (M + 1) \times (50) - (50)$$
$$125 = (50M + 50)$$
$$75 = 50M$$
$$1.5 = M$$

Thus, with the 75mm extension and 50mm lens, your subject would appear 1.5 times life-sized on your film.

A more direct method of calculating magnification is by simple measurement. If you place a ruler in the subject plane and note the number of inches or millimeters you can see in your viewer, you need only compare this measurement to the size of the film format. A 35mm frame is about 1" x 1½" (24mm x 36mm). Thus, if 1½" of the ruler appears along the long dimension of the frame, the magnification is 1x; if 3 inches appears, .50x; and so on. In the long run, keeping track of your magnifications is a good idea to help you label your slides. More immediately, it is a working necessity because your exposure must be adjusted to allow for lens extension.

Recall from the chapter on *The Camera's Controls* that light diminishes in direct proportion to the square of the distance traveled. Thus, if you add extension tubes or extend your bellows to a distance equal to the focal length of your lens, the light will be traveling twice as far as normal, and its intensity will be reduced to ¼ strength. An exposure increase of 4x will be necessary to compensate for the extension. A built-in meter will eliminate the need for mental gymnastics, but an awareness and understanding of the necessary exposure increase can assist you in choosing a sufficiently fast film to allow for action-stopping shutter speeds or small apertures for maximum depth of field. Without through-the-lens metering you must do the exposure calculations in your head. The accompanying ruler offers a quick and handy working

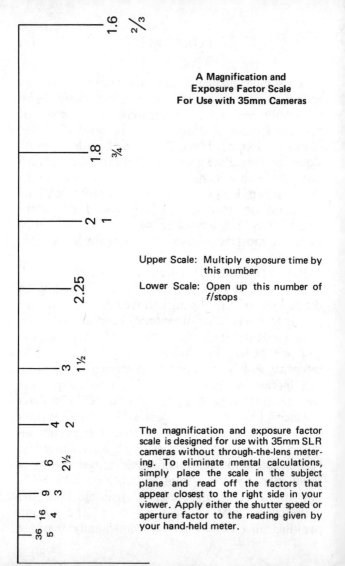

**A Magnification and
Exposure Factor Scale
For Use with 35mm Cameras**

Upper Scale: Multiply exposure time by this number

Lower Scale: Open up this number of f/stops

The magnification and exposure factor scale is designed for use with 35mm SLR cameras without through-the-lens metering. To eliminate mental calculations, simply place the scale in the subject plane and read off the factors that appear closest to the right side in your viewer. Apply either the shutter speed or aperture factor to the reading given by your hand-held meter.

1.6 2/3

1.8 3/4

2 1

2.25

3 1½

4 2

6 2½

9 3

16 4

36 5

method. Simply poke it, instead of a standard ruler, into your picture at the subject plane, read off the necessary increase, and adjust the setting given by your light meter accordingly.

Exposure adjustments can be mathematically calculated by using the following formula:

$$\frac{\text{(length of lens + length of extension)}^2}{\text{Length of lens}^2} =$$

exposure factor

For example, if you were using the lens and extension cited above — a 50mm lens plus 50mm extension — the calculations would run this way:

$$\frac{(50 + 50)^2}{50^2} = \text{exposure factor}$$

$$\frac{10000}{2500} = 4$$

Macro Lenses

A macro lens is designed for making extreme close-ups, or "photomacrographs," of subjects at close range. It will focus much closer than an ordinary lens of the same focal length without any accessory equipment; but it can also be used at normal distances and will focus all the way to infinity. Allowing for the quick shift from normal

to close-up photographs without any fuss or
bother, a macro is a worthwhile investment if you
aim to take a good number of close-ups.

Roses Are Red, Sometimes

The same subtle shifts in the color of natural
daylight, which lend a sense of mood and atmosphere to your landscape pictures, will give a
distinct color cast to your close-ups. White flowers
photographed on an overcast day in a shadowy
spot will be pale blue in your picture; red ones,
cerise; pink ones, lavender. Photographing your
samples at high noon when the light is most evenly
balanced will produce truer colors, but in high
contrast, with bright highlights and harsh shadows
— a visual effect often incompatible with your
subject. Thus, close-up photography becomes the
area of nature shooting in which the photographer
may most often wish to adjust the available light or
disregard it entirely.

To adjust the color of the natural light, you can
use a warming filter to get rid of the blue tinge.
White cardboard or tinfoil reflectors, placed so the
sun will strike them and they, in turn, will bounce
the light onto your subject and provide fill-in light,
can help to bring deep shadow areas within the
contrast range of your film. Even a small pocket
mirror can be used like a mini-spotlight to reflect

the sunlight onto the subject.

Portable light units, both flash guns and electronic flash, can be used as the main light source for outdoor shooting. Electronic flash, with its extremely fast sunlight-balanced burst of light, is a godsend in stopping the action of close-up flower or insect subjects.

You can use articificial light in the field with all the imagination and ingenuity that you might employ indoors. Handsome back-lit or cross-lit shots are possible. If you wish to use artificial light only for fill, make your reading and exposure for the existing natural light, and position your light at twice the normal light-to-subject distance or quench its brightness with a fewer layers of white handkerchief.

Strobe units match daylight and assure correct color rendition with daylight color films. If you use flash, choose blue flash bulbs or flash cubes to produce natural results on daylight film. If you use clear flash bulbs you must either use films balanced for tungsten light or a filter that subtracts some of the red from the flash. As always, filtering will necessitate an exposure increase, and with shallow depth of field and necessary fast shutter speeds — the twin facts of life in close-up work — the last thing you'll want to do is to introduce anything that will mean opening up the lens or slowing the shutter speed any more than is already necessary.

Lighting Set-ups for Outdoor Close-ups

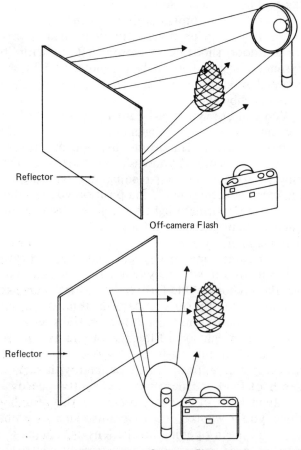

Reflector

Off-camera Flash

Reflector

On-camera Flash

Lighting Set-ups for Outdoor Close-ups

Advanced amateur and professional photographers often bring artificial light sources into the field for close-up work. Flash or strobe units provide balanced color lighting to assure correct color rendition no matter what the natural lighting conditions are. And, a burst of bright artificial light can often allow you to use a smaller aperture in combination with a motion-stopping shutter speed. Finally, if the position of the artificial light unit is judiciously thought out, handsome studio-style effects can be achieved. The illustrations opposite show two basic lighting positions. If the flash or strobe unit is attached to the camera, the light will be frontal. An angled reflector positioned to the side, rear, and out of the lens' view will reflect some of the light back onto the side of the subject. If off-camera flash or strobe is positioned high and behind the subject, with the reflector in front of the subject next to the camera, the backlighting will create a handsome rimlight effect around the subject. And enough light will be reflected off the foreground reflector to light the front of the subject.

Flash Exposure Chart for Close-ups
For ASA 64 Films

Flashbulb and Reflector	Lens Opening	
	Subject Distance 10-20 inches	Subject Distance: 30 inches
Flashcube or Supercube	f/16	f/11
Hi-Power or Hi-Output cube	f/22	f/16
AG-1B, shallow cylindrical reflector	f/16	f/11
AG-1B, polished-bowl reflector	f/22	f/16
M2B, polished-bowl reflector	f/22	f/16
M3B, 5B, or 25B, polished-bowl reflector	f/22 (with two layers of handkerchiefs)	f/22

Electronic Flash Exposure Chart for Close-ups
For ASA 64 Films

Output of Unit BCPS	Lens Opening	
	Subject Distance: 10-20 inches	Subject Distance: 30 inches
700-1000	f/16	f/8
1000-2000	f/16	f/11
2800-4000	f/22	f/16
5600-8000	f/22 (with two layers of handkerchiefs)	f/22

The charts opposite give f/stop settings based on the flashbulb and reflector in use or the light-output rating of the electronic-flash unit. Exposures should be made with one layer of white handkerchief over the light unit to avoid harshness. For flashbulbs the shutter speed should be 1/25 or 1/30th sec. For electronic flash, the shutter speed on focal-plane shutter cameras must be set at the electronic-flash-synchronization setting. With leaf-type shutters and electronic flash, any shutter speed can be used.

The f/stops given are for such ASA 64 films as Kodak Ektachrome-X, Kodachrome-X, or Ektacolor-X. If an ASA 25 film, such as Kodachrome II, is used, open up one stop over the indicated settings.

An Outdoor Studio

Thus far this book has more or less ignored the techniques and tricks of studio and commercial photographers. But your results in close-up photography can be enhanced by the introduction of some simple studio techniques into the field.

An inexpensive glass aquarium can serve you well as a portable outdoor studio. It will confine small reptiles and insects so that you can lend your full attention to photographing rather than chasing them. And it can serve as the perfect staging area for shoreside underwater photographs of small specimens. To prepare your set, scoop up some earth, pebbles, shells, or plant life appropriate to your subject and its environment. Blank out the view through the aquarium by placing a solid-colored cardboard or cloth behind it or by painting the back wall in advance. Blue or green backgrounds look most natural. Black produces a dramatic, but unnatural, effect and makes any debris obvious if your setup contains water and marine subjects. You can leave the back wall clear or uncovered if you wish, as the background setting seen through the aquarium will be entirely out of focus. If this is the case, be sure to position the setup so as to not include any strong visual element – the shape of a tree will be maintained even out of focus – or sunlight shining through from the rear, which would complicate exposure and lighting considerations. If you have provided natural props, and not treated your subjects roughly in transferring them to the aquarium, they should become acclimated in a few minutes. Wait for them to resume their normal routines before beginning.

Light for your mini-studio can be provided either by the natural sunlight entering from above or by artificial lighting. Never shoot with your flash or strobe square on or you'll only record the bright flash of light bouncing off the glass. Also, beware of glints from your camera reflecting off the front of the aquarium and showing up in the picture. To guard against this, cut a hole in a piece of dark cardboard just large enough for the front of your lens to poke through and work through this masking; or place your lens flush up against the glass.

In the controlled environment of the aquarium

you can fight the limitations of the shallow, close-up depth of field by herding your subjects into a space toward the front side. Gentle prodding should do for most reptiles and insects, while a sheet of glass dropped vertically down into the water works quite well in limiting the fore-to-aft mobility of small fish.

With the proper care in setting up your scene, placing your lights (or positioning your setup if sunlight is the light source), and careful handling of your subjects, the introduction of basic studio techniques into your outdoor work need not detract from the naturalism of your results.

The Birds and the Beasts

A nature photographer must necessarily develop the same knowledge and skills as a hunter, but without the lethal effects. Both depend for success on awareness of the whereabouts and behavior of wildlife, the technique of stalking, the placement of effective blinds, and the equipment to be used.

Where and When to Find Your Subjects

The where and when of animal photography depends on the types of animals you hope to find. Wildlife directories are available from national and regional groups. They will prove helpful in locating and identifying subjects. Invariably, your local ornithological organizations are helpful in dispensing information on the breeding and nesting times of indigenous birds and the migration periods of the more exotic species that pass through your region annually. Away from home, local residents are often happy to describe the native fauna to interested visitors, and professional guides and rangers are to be found in the most popular touring and camping areas. However, distance or any exotic subject are not necessary factors in capturing interesting animal photographs. A nearby marsh, a small wood, or even a backyard with a few trees may well prove to be a fertile starting ground for your animal and bird photography. Some classic animal photographs have even been taken in zoos.

Animal and Human Behavior

Once you have located your subjects, some knowledge of their behavior, coupled with sympathetic behavior on your part, will lead to successful and interesting pictures. Stealth is as much a part of the photo-hunter's bag of tricks as camera and lens are. Dress appropriately in snug clothing of a drab color. Avoid carrying anything that jangles or reflects brightly in the sun. Move through underbrush, or whatever cover nature affords, slowly and quietly. If you establish a blind or lookout, keep your activity around it to the absolute minimum. Stock it before hand with sufficient film, water, snacks, insect repellant, and whatever else you can imagine needing. This will eliminate unnecessary trips in and out of the blind.

Beware of mating males and new mothers. Even non-aggressive animals are unpredictable at such times. Never disturb a mother and her newborn. She may either turn on you to drive you off or be so disconcerted by your intrusion as to run off herself, abandoning her young. Photographers are often tempted to approach the nests of birds too close and too abruptly. You may find yourself dive-bombed by an angry mother if you succumb to that temptation. Or, the frightened mother may never return to her nest.

With a little time and patience in approaching a bird's nest, the breeding site, the feeding spot of a small mammal, or even the watering place of a larger species, you may well win acceptance as some strange but unthreatening part of the total scene. You will be repaid with good pictures without endangering yourself or your subjects.

The Long Lens – An Absolute Necessity

A long, or telephoto, lens is the *sine qua non* of wildlife photography. Most of your pictures will be taken at a considerable distance from your subjects, and to achieve those frame-filling animal portraits that you've doubtless admired in travel, wildlife, and photographic magazines, you'll need a lens in the 300mm range. This purchase will be a major addition to your equipment kit. It is bound to be expensive. Good telephoto lenses are not cheap, and the least expensive ones are usually inferior. But shop around. You don't have to buy the most expensive ones to get good quality. Telephoto lenses may often be purchased second-hand. Check the listings in the classified pages of your local newspaper or consult your camera shop about used equipment. Never accept a used lens or any other used equipment without an absolute guarantee that it may be returned if you find it defective.

The tele-extenders described earlier may well seem the answer to the problem of increased focal length at minimum cost. Indeed they are if animal and bird photography are to remain a sometime thing with you and the price of a long lens seems truly extreme in reference to how little use you intend to make of it. But remember the limitations of the tele-extenders: diminished light transmission and decreased optical performance. If you hope to do a good deal of wildlife photography, there is simply no way around the purchase of a good long lens.

Using Your Telephoto

The chapter on *The Camera's Controls* points out the relationship between depth of field and focal length. Bear in mind that the area of acceptable sharp focus in your picture will become very shallow with a long-focal-length lens. Focusing must be exact, and with moving subjects exact focus must be achieved quickly. Practice zeroing in on this and that around home or camp until focusing becomes almost reflexive. Some long lenses, specially designed for animal and action work, allow for focusing by simply sliding the front elements forward and backward rather than rotating, as with standard lenses.

Remember, too, that long lenses simply do not come with nice big apertures to allow plenty of light for focusing. Many of the super-telephotos offer a maximum aperture of only $f/8$! The image in your viewer may be dim even at maximum aperture. If your ground-glass focusing screen has a central split-image focusing device, you may discover that half of it goes dark when a long lens is used, and you are left to try lining up half your subject with nothing but a black semicircle. If the ground glass in your prism or camera is removable, it can be replaced with one specially designed for low-light or long-lens viewing.

Long lenses need support even at fast shutter speeds. A tripod, monopod, or shoulder pod should be used. Lacking any of these, the shoulders of a cooperative and crouching friend or mate, a nearby rock, or even a tree trunk will provide some insurance against camera shake.

In attempting to master the exact focusing and steady exposure release necessary with a long lens, and when you add tracking a moving subject to the list of problems, you probably produced pictures at first that demonstrate the impossibility of the situation. Persist. And if you're planning a trip or wildlife photography expedition, master these necessary skills before you set out.

Photographic Blinds

Blinds are an asset to the wildlife photographer in allowing him to approach his photographic quarry closely and without detection. An automobile, tent, or even some camouflage material simply draped over the photographer, all can serve as improptu blinds. Directions for the building of a comfortable, well-ventilated, lightweight blind that can be easily carried even to a relatively unaccessible territory and erected in a few minutes time are given in the accompanying diagram and instructions.

The location of the blind must be carefully considered. Even the most artful disguise will not conceal your presence from animals if your blind and you are located upwind from them. Activity around and about the blind or noise emanating from it will alert the animal to your presence. One interesting fact to remember about birds and blinds: birds seem incapable of counting. If two figures enter a blind and then one leaves, the birds will accept the blind and its remaining inhabitant-photographer without concern.

Animals are extremely wary of any foreign intrusion. Even if you remain undetected, the sound of your camera may startle them. And, they can respond *very* quickly — appearing as a blur at slow shutter settings. Use a fast shutter speed and wrap your camera in some muffling material or

An Easy-to-Assemble Light-Weight Blind

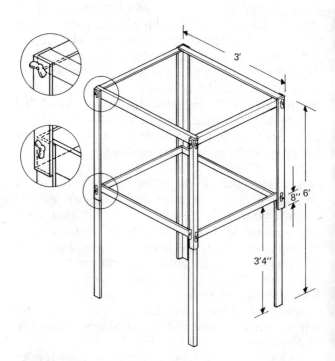

To construct a light-weight blind, cut and assemble "L"-shaped aluminum. The structure can be held together with ½" or ¼" bolts. The covering is made from two lengths of burlap, canvas or nylon (pre-shrunk or washed before sewing), with three sides sewn

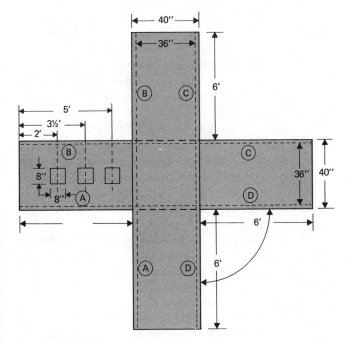

together and a zipper inserted in the fourth. With an evening's work you'll own a sturdy blind that bundles up into a package only 3'4" long and about 1'6" in diameter.

even a towel, or encase it in a specially designed "blimp" to eliminate noise.

While touring wildlife preserves and refuges by car, or even if you simply spot some interesting animal subject while driving along, your car can serve as a quite adequate roadside blind.

When photographing from a moving vehicle never lean your camera or upper body against the car itself for support, you'll only pick up the motor vibrations and ruin any potential picture you may have. Instead, hold the camera firmly to your eye with your elbows tucked well in against your body. In this way you employ your body as a cushioning spring to absorb the car's vibration. Or, better still, make yourself a small beanbag or sandbag — loosely packed — and use that as a cushion between the camera and vehicle.

Recall the rules about motion and camera-to-subject distance as outlined in the chapter on *The Camera's Controls.* Your motion, its speed and direction, are as important for a clear picture as is the motion of your subject. If you are working a subject at close range from a moving vehicle going even 10 or 15 miles per hour, you'll need a very fast shutter speed to record anything more than a worthless blur. A distant group of animals in a landscape setting can be recorded quite satisfactorily with you traveling at greater speeds and shooting at slower shutter speeds. Remember, too, that using a telephoto essentially reduces the distance between you and your subject. With really long lenses the car should be stopped while you make your exposures; otherwise, if the motion doesn't blur your picture, the motor vibration most probably will.

Remote Shutter Releases

Remote releases offer the wildlife photographer the advantage of being able to set up his camera close to his subjects and then withdraw to an acceptable distance from which to trigger his exposures. The simpler releases are mechanical, activated by the photographer from his vantage point. More sophisticated releases are activated by the subjects themselves.

Mechanical Releases

An improvised lever, which will at the jerk of a cord depress the camera's shutter release, is the simplest sort of remote release. The photographer needs only set up his camera near a game trail, watering hole, or bird's nest, frame an area of probable activity, and withdraw. Watching the action from a distance either with the unaided eye or through binoculars, he need only tug a string to drop the lever and take the picture.

The technique of using a cable or air-pressure

release is similar. Cable releases are available in lengths up to 12 feet — long enough for photographing a bird's nest or small mammals, but an impossibly and dangerously short one photographing for big game. Air releases are available in lengths up to 200 feet. Pressure, created by squeezing a rubber ball at the photographer's end of the tube, travels along and activates a plunger at the shutter. For long-distance work, a small bicycle pump should be used instead of the rubber ball to create a good burst of pressure that will surely activate the shutter. Rubber tubing has been known to stretch, dissipating the pressure, so for use over long distances, plastic tubing is best.

Electrical Releases

The camera shutter can be activated from even greater distances than those mentioned above by the use of a simple electrical circuit. In the field you'll need a battery pack, wiring, a switch of some sort, and a device called a solenoid. The solenoid exerts a force when the electrical circuit is closed. Attached to your shutter release, it will set off your camera.

The switch in your line can be a common electrical switch, activated by the photographer from his vantage point or by the subjects themselves. A pressure mat, mousetrap, or electric eye will have your subjects taking their own pictures.

True "Remote" Releases

Beyond the distance they allow the photographer to establish between himself and his wary or dangerous subjects, remotes offer other advantages. As the camera can be positioned close to the potential subject, shorter focal lenses than usual for wildlife shots can be used (and shorter focal length means increased depth of field). As the camera must be positioned out of the way of animal traffic, the Rowi clamp is ideal for use with a remote release, allowing the camera to be clamped to a tree branch for a nice, high, unobstructed view point and maximum safety from being disturbed.

Lighting units can be coupled to your camera for night shots, just as they would be coupled for routine shooting. If you are using color film, be sure to choose an emulsion appropriate to your intended light source. "Daylight" color films are used with electronic flash or blue flash bulbs. Clear flash bulbs produce a reddish light and must be used only with tungsten color films. Color-matching considerations are not necessary when using panchromatic black-and-white films.

If the camera is to be left out overnight, protect it properly despite even the most ironclad reassurances from the weatherman. Wrap the camera in plastic sheeting or enclose it in a plastic bag. Make certain that the wrapping is held snugly in place. A

A Photo-electric Camera Trap

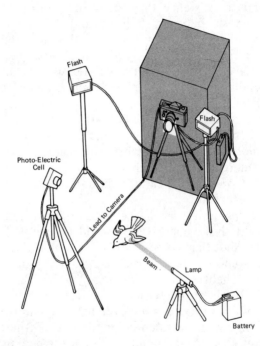

When the light beam from the battery-powered lamp to the photo-electric cell is broken by the presence of an animal subject, the shutter is released and the two flash lamps are tripped. In the drawing, the lamp, cell, and light units are placed at ground level. They could be clamped instead to tree branches, with the camera trained on a high-up nest.

piece of flapping plastic will warn subjects that something's up, and undo your best-laid plans.

The major problem in using remote releases with conventional equipment is the necessity to return to the camera after each exposure to advance the film and recock the shutter. As surreptitiously as this task may be performed, it will alert the animals in the area to your presence. The resolution to the resetting problem, alas, lies in a piece of equipment that — owing to its high price — must remain a dream to most photographers: a motor drive. With a motor-driven camera, the current, generated when your subject trips your photo-trap, will take the picture, recock the shutter, advance the film, and take frame after frame as long as the current is maintained. Standard rolls of 36 exposures as well as loads of 250 and 800 exposures that allow for the camera to be left unattended for days (depending on the animal traffic) are available for special motor-driven camera backs.

Animal Portraiture

The finest animal photographs are essentially portraits. Some preliminary research will do more than help you find your subjects; it will help you be alert to the photographic possibilities once you've found them. Characteristics of behavior, some special (and usually vital) adaptation that a certain animal may possess, group activities of animals at various stages of development, feeding, mating, and so forth, all provide natural picture-taking possibilities. It falls to you the photographer to come equipped with more than a camera; you should also have a knowledge of what makes your subject special.

Close-up portraits of larger mammals can be achieved with your long lens. Initially, the mere presence of your subject looming in your viewer may generate the temptation to make your exposure without first considering the pictorial possibilities. Just a moment after your photograph that big cat with his head down and his eyes lost in pockets of deep shadow, he may well raise his head to put his face in full sunshine, or yawn, or blink, or swat a fly off his nose. A moment's hesitation plus some portrait-photography thinking will, more often than not, add up to pictures that do more than just prove you were there.

A Final Word About Birds

Birds are among the most popular nature photography subjects; and as subjects go, they're rough. A roll or two of blurs, half birds, birds taken just a moment too early or too late, can so disillusion the most bird-loving photographer as to give rise to thoughts of abandoning the whole thing or taking up landscape photography instead. But take heart, Rome wasn't built in a day — and so forth.

Birds, like all photo subjects, must be considered in reference to both technical and pictorial aspects. The long lens is a necessity, and its shallow depth of field, that ever-present bugaboo, a definite liability. How then can one even hope to focus on a single bird with all the sky to swoop around in — and swooping around in all that sky as if to torment a poor photographer? Remember, focus exists in a plane a certain distance from the camera. Choose a bird flying parallel to you and your camera. To counteract the blur that will be produced by the bird's motion across your frame, move your camera at his pace to hold him steady in your view. When you make your exposure, remember to keep moving the camera. It does no good to track the subject, then halt abruptly and take the picture. Unless you stay with the subject through the picture-taking, you'll record an off-center bird, or worse — tail feathers.

Consider the bird in relation to the entire frame. You may wish to position his outstretched wings on the diagonal or record him off-center to create a sort of flying space in front of him. Empty space behind the bird is usually a tip-off to poor tracking or delayed shutter release.

Perching birds present fewer problems. You should approach prudently and focus swiftly so as neither to scare the bird off nor give him a chance to fly away just as you've finally found perfect focus. Birds will perch on certain branches or rocks with endearing regularity, if undisturbed. Keep an eye out, and you may notice that the same bird will stop on the same lookout branch on every trip to and from the nest or that a certain group of seabirds arrives on a certain shoreside rock every day at supper time. Prefocus on the perching point, wait, and when the subjects arrive, shoot.

Underwater Photography

The world beneath the sea has always fascinated man, and even before the turn of the century an adventuresome French zoologist, Louis Boutan, took himself and his camera underwater to record this previously unknown region and its often-mis-understood creatures. His equipment was bulky and his films slow, and he himself was limited in range and mobility by the cumbersome diving gear of the times. His results were astonishing, but more as curiosities than as nature studies.

Underwater photography remained as something of an oddity until the availability of a practical self-contained underwater breathing apparatus (scuba) after World War II. Scuba gear freed man to move around underwater with fishlike agility and extended the range and duration of his forays. Films had improved in the decades that passed since Boutan's first shots. And, camera and equipment manufacturers responded to underwater needs by producing lines of protective, watertight camera housings. Thus, a whole new kind of nature photography was born, nearly fifty years after its conception.

The variety of underwater photography is as generous as the variety above water — and the same care must be taken not to disturb or damage the environment. Plants, animals, and landscapes all await the informed photographer. Landside preparation and the ability to identify your subjects and anticipate their behavior may not only gain you a picture, it may save your life.

No one should casually attempt skin diving for the first time while on vacation, no matter how attractive the displays of rental equipment may be. A thorough course given by a professional or expert diver is an absolute prerequisite to your first outing. And, some background, armchair study of the subjects you'll find underwater is the only way to prepare yourself for differentiating between harmless and potentially harmful specimens.

Cameras and Housings

Any brand or model of camera can be used underwater, so long as it is encased in a waterproof container or housing. Some photographers favor 35mm cameras for underwater work because they allow for at least 36 exposures without the necessity of surfacing to reload. This becomes a real consideration on deep dives, when surfacing must be done gradually. The 2¼" reflex cameras offer the advantage of the large ground-glass viewing screen for checking your focus and framing. Despite the limit of 12 to 20 frames per standard load, they are underwater favorites.

Housings are available in both plastic and metal and in a great range of prices. For a beginner who doesn't expect to make deep dives or do too much underwater work, the least expensive type of case that will accommodate his camera will do fine. But if you are bitten by the underwater bug, that inexpensive first housing may prove a false bargain. The more expensive cases are simply better designed to withstand pressure at greater depths and to simplify the operation and adjustment of your camera underwater. The less wasted space within your housing, the less ballast necessary to keep it submerged. Lightweight plastic housings invariably need weight added to sink them, but they will float if dropped overboard accidentally. The heavier metal housings require no ballasts, are more rugged, but cost more.

One solution to the housing problem is to have a camera that is completely watertight; another, to have a camera and films that are impervious to salt water. Nikon offers the Nikonos, a watertight and pressure-resistant 35mm camera designed for use both under and above water, while the Navy, directing its research in just the opposite direction, is presently testing a camera that simply fills with water upon immersion and takes its pictures on film that is not harmed by the water.

Light

Light, that ever prime ingredient of photography, is greatly changed by its passage through water. Swimming freely underwater, the novice may allow his enthusiasm to blind him to the changes – until he is made aware of them in his pictures. The light is dimmer down below because of the filtering effect of the water, and objects appear larger, closer, and blue. Unless the effects of water upon light are taken into account, portions of the subject will be chopped off, the resulting pictures will be underexposed, and colors will be washed out or lost altogether.

Refraction of Light

As light passes from one medium to another of a different density its rays are refracted, or bent, and the image is enlarged or diminished according to the relative densities of the two media. As the light from your underwater subject passes from water into the less dense air in your camera housing, it speeds up and is refracted outward, making underwater subjects appear closer and larger than they are in fact. This refraction increases image size, shortening the apparent camera-to-subject distance by approximately 1/3.

Focusing and framing must be done on the basis of the *apparent* – rather than the actual – subject distance. You can trust your eye underwater be-

Refraction Effects Underwater

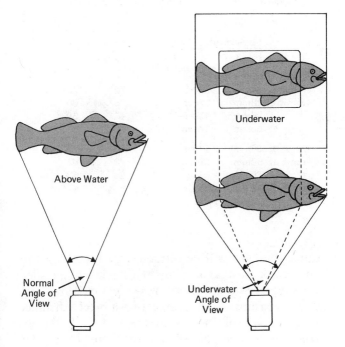

As the drawings show, objects underwater appear closer and larger than they would at a similar distance above water. The first drawing shows a fish as it would be reproduced photographed above water at a certain distance. The second drawing shows what would happen if the above-water shooting distance was maintained while photographing the same subject underwater. It would be rendered larger and go beyond the edges of the frame. Underwater you must focus on the apparent camera-to-subject distance.

Changes in Angle of View and Focal Length Underwater

	Focal length of lens		Angle of view	
	above water	underwater	above water	underwater
35mm cameras	21mm	28mm	92°	75°
	28mm	37mm	75°	60°
	35mm	47mm	63°	50°
	50mm	67mm	47°	36°
2¼ x 2¼ cameras	38mm	51mm	93°	77°
	50mm	67mm	78°	62°
	60mm	80mm	68°	53°
	80mm	106mm	53°	41°

cause the light will be refracted by the air in your face mask, just as it is by the air in your camera housing. If you are shooting critical close-ups, and you measure your camera-to-subject distance, subtract 1/3 of the distance to establish the distance at which you should set your focus. The working focal length and angle of view of your lens will be affected, so that a 50mm lens underwater will perform much as a longer 67mm lens performs out of the water. Wide-angle lenses are favorites for underwater shooting because they perform like normal lenses and increase depth of field, minimizing focusing errors.

Surface Reflections

Even the calmest sea will reflect some of the light striking the surface. The amount of reflection is greatest when the sun is at a low angle — in the early morning or late afternoon. And choppy surface will reflect more light than a smooth one. So, the best shooting time for underwater photography is from two hours before through two hours after noon on a calm day.

Light Scattering

Despite its fluidity, and the ease with which we can move through it, water is 800 times denser than air, as anyone who has ever been clouted by a good-sized wave will attest. It also contains a good quantity of matter — microscopic plant and animal life, sand, minerals, among other things. The amount of suspended matter in the water is greater as one approaches the poles. Thus, water in temperate regions is less clear than water in tropical regions. Both the water molecules and the suspended particles affect the light. The light is literally *scattered* as it strikes the molecules and matter and bounces off in a new direction. Scattering causes underwater light to become diffused and non-directional, lowering contrast and eliminating shadows that help to define objects in above-water photography. The deeper you go or the more turbid the water, the greater the scattering and the less definition in your photograph. In addition, the blue portion of natural sunlight is scattered more than the red, lending an overall blue tint to your picture. Scattering occurs along the path of any light ray traveling underwater — in any direction. It is not only a function of depth, it also occurs along the distance between your camera and subject. To obtain good contrast in your pictures, you must work from a reasonably short camera-to-subject distance. Even at shallow depths in the clearest water, definition will be lost in pictures taken at camera-to-subject distances greater than about 10 feet.

Light Absorption

Absorption produces the most profound effect on color underwater. The longer wavelengths at the "warm" end of the spectrum (reds and oranges) are absorbed more than the short, "cool" wavelengths (blues and greens). The deeper or the farther away from your subject you go, the less evident bright reds and oranges will be. Even at a depth or camera-to-subject distance of 15 feet in the clearest water, red will be reproduced as a dull brown, and at 30 feet it will have lost its color entirely, whereas blue and green objects will be reproduced naturally.

Filters, useful in correcting light imbalances above water, will have some corrective effect underwater as long as a color is not completely gone.

Refraction and Absorption Underwater

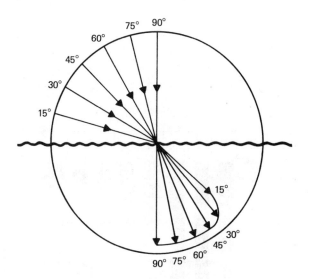

This diagram illustrates the refraction and absorption effects of
sunlight passing through water. Refraction occurs at the surface
when the light passes into the water. Because water is denser than
air, the light rays are actually bent. Absorption occurs as the light
travels through the water. In effect, the intensity of the light is
diminished the farther it travels underwater. Light from directly
overhead, as at noon, will travel the shortest distance to reach a
certain underwater depth. Light rays entering water at angles of less
than 90 degrees, as in the early morning or late afternoon, will travel
farther to reach a given depth. The relative strength of rays entering
at the various angles and passing to a given underwater depth is
indicated by the length of the lines underwater.

Selective Absorption of Light Underwater

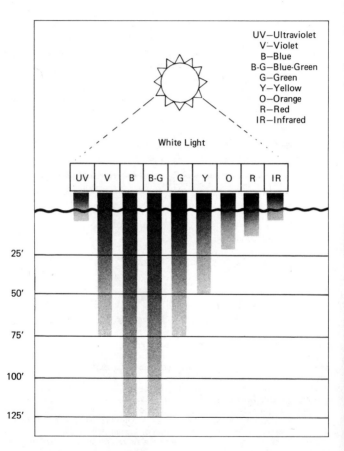

The drawing opposite shows the effects of selective absorption of certain portions of the spectrum underwater. Ultraviolet and infrared rays are the first lost. Then come red and orange — completely gone at a depth of 25 feet. The other colors are absorbed completely at various depths until nothing is left except blue and green.

They will do nothing to restore the reds, oranges, and yellows to your underwater color shots taken at depths or distances greater than 30 feet. The water itself acts like a filter, affecting the light before it reaches you or your subject. A filter can only accentuate certain colors and diminish others; there is no way filtration can restore color that has been removed. Using a filter in the hope of restoring the lost reds and oranges will only restrain the blues and greens, necessitating a longer exposure in an already low-light situation, while producing no positive effect at all. But all is not lost.

Artificial Light

The underwater use of artificial lighting, be it strobe or simple flash bulbs, solves the problems of diminished light intensity and color imbalance. In bringing your own light source along with you, you are essentially carrying a personal packet of sunshine to whatever depth you wish to descend. But remember that scattering and absorption will affect your artificial light source just as they affect natural light. Keep shooting distances to a minimum for sharp definition and good color rendition. The light will pass through water both on its way to your subject and on its way back, so even at a shooting distance of 5 feet you'll begin to lose your reds and pick up an overall blue tone again, despite the use of artificial light. For shooting distances greater than 5 feet, you may wish to use clear flash bulbs, which ordinarily would produce overly reddish results on your daylight color film. The filtering effect of water will counteract the reddishness of the clear bulbs and produce normal-looking results underwater.

The suspended particles in water will do more than diffuse and absorb your artificial light. If the light is mounted on the camera, the rays will strike the particles directly and be reflected, just as headlights are reflected back by a dense fog. This backscattering will register the particles on your film as out-of-focus light spots or an overall haze, and mar definition and contrast in your subject. You can reduce backscatter by positioning your flash above and to side of your camera.

Flash Exposure

Above-water flash exposure is based on a system of guide numbers. The guide number for a certain flash bulb or electronic-flash unit indicates its strength as rated by the manufacturer. To determine correct exposure at a shutter setting appropriate to your light unit, divide the guide number by the camera-to-subject distance to discover the correct f/stop. For instance, with a guide number of 40 and a shooting distance of 10 feet the correct f/stop would be f/4. With the same guide number, 40, and a shooting distance of only 5 feet, the f/stop would be f/8. Underwater, again taking into consideration diffusion and absorption, you must reduce the rated number of your flash or strobe. Even in the clearest, calmest water, divide it by 3 before proceeding with your camera-to-subject calculations. Under less than clear and calm circumstances, divide by 4. As the degree of turbidity and amount of suspended matter are difficult to gauge by eye, you'll do well to bracket your underwater shots to insure results. Make one exposure at the calculated setting, *plus* one stop under and one stop over. If this seems wasteful of film now, it will not seem so the first time you discover that your supposedly under- or overexposed picture is the one that reproduces the scene or subject just as you wish it reproduced.

Underwater Light Effects

Artificial lighting can be used as creatively below water as above. Sidelighting will emphasize textures in interesting surfaces. Flat frontal lighting in photographs taken in open water with the camera parallel to the water surface will cause your subject to seem to float in front of a black velvet backdrop as the light that passes the subject will continue on and not be reflected back to the lens. Frontal lighting of translucent subjects will make them seem opaque, while top-, side-, or backlighting will emphasize their translucence. A subject taken from below, with the sun-struck surface behind it, will appear against a bright, dappled blue backdrop. Auxiliary, fill lighting is necessary in such shots to counteract the imbalance of backlighting and hold detail in the near side of the subject.

Care, Display, and Presentation of Photographs

A shooting vacation may well yield a hundred or even a thousand negatives and transparencies you wish to preserve, while a year or a lifetime can produce a jumbled heap unless you, early on, make a practice of recording and storing your materials with one eye toward classification and the other toward preservation. Such a cross-eyed approach will make your material ever retrievable and assure that it will be in good condition.

Negatives, Slides, and Prints

Negatives and slides are still film, and they should be stored and handled with the care that film demands. Kept in a cool, dry place, they will be safe for years. Negatives should be contact printed and then placed in glassine envelopes specially made to fit every format. Keeping the contact sheets in a ring binder, with the envelope of appropriate negatives taped to the back of each, is a simple, straightforward filing system.

A similar system works well for slides. Plastic sheets are available for all popular sizes of color transparencies. The slides are simply slipped into slots in the sheets, which are prepunched for ring binder filing. Sheets can be made for each shooting or, as times go by, you may wish to refile your slides by subject. Once in their envelope or plastic sheet, negatives and transparencies are protected from dust and dirt, fingerprints, and scratches – all of which can ruin them.

Prints can always be duplicated, but that's no reason to abuse them. If you print up your own enlargements, the boxes from your printing paper make good, sturdy files. If your prints are processed by a commercial lab, you need simply ask for some empty boxes, which would otherwise be thrown away. Displayed prints are safer behind glass, protected from airborne dust and dirt, yellowing cigarette smoke, and whatever other pollutants your personal atmosphere may contain. Well-processed black-and-white prints are stable and usually unaffected by light; but color prints will bleach out if exposed to prolonged direct sunlight. Hang your black and whites where you please, but reserve those spaces between the sun-bright windows or in shady nooks for your color prints.

Mounting and Framing Prints

You can mount and frame your prints at home at reasonable expense and with professional results.

Dry-mounting tissue is available at photography and art-supply stores. It resembles waxed paper. When you place it between your print and mounting board and apply heat to the sandwich, it simply melts and binds your print *permanently* to its backing. It should be the only thing you use to mount your prints. Glues or rubber cement may seem easier at first, but a print, ruined by stains or bubbles after a few months time, will cancel out whatever time or expense you saved.

To dry mount your pictures, start by tacking a piece of tissue to the back of the photo by applying heat. Then trim the print and tissue. Next, place the trimmed photo and tissue on your board, position them as you wish, and iron the print, working from the center out. (The print should be covered with a smooth sheet of clean thick cardboard during ironing.) Finally, trim the board to leave a margin − or none if you wish.

Framing has become simplicity itself since the introduction of handsome, adjustable, standard-sized photo frames. The simplest device is made of two brackets that clamp your mounted photo and protective glass together at the top and bottom. The distance between the brackets can be adjusted to accommodate any size picture. Simple plastic boxes are also available as frames. They come in 5" x 7", 8" x 10", 11" x 14", and 16" x 20" sizes. You drop in your print and insert a frame-filling cardboard box behind it. Perforations in the back of the cardboard permit vertical or horizontal hanging; all you need is a nail. More expensive, but still reasonably priced, are precut metal frames in dull aluminum or bright chrome, brass or color finishes. You join three sides of the frame with the L-brackets provided, slip in your glass and print, and, finally, the last side of the frame, and you have framed your print just as you've seen prints framed in museums and galleries.

Organizing a Slide Show

The day is bound to come when you wish to show your slides — to friends, a nature-study group, a photo club, or a potential buyer. The key word in getting together an interesting and smooth-running show is *organization.* You can best begin by editing each roll of slides as soon as you get it back from the processor. If you ever have the opportunity to watch a professional sort his take, you may be dumbfounded as he spreads box after box of newly processed slides out on a light box and then whips through them as quickly as if he were sorting beans. The selects will probably go into a small neat pile, the rejects into the wastebasket. If you protest, he will probably explain that if he did not like them the first time, he would not like them the second — and, he will be right.

Such editing overkill is not really necessary, especially at first, but you should go through your slides, choose the best, and separate them from the set. Save the extras, near dupes, and second choices in the slide boxes, labeled, of course, and store the choices in your plastic sheets. When the time comes to organize your show, you need only hold up the sheet to the light or view it on a light box to see what you've got. Rearrange the slides in the sheets or on the light box to set up an interesting visual or storytelling sequence. Then stand them all up on end, upside down, as they will go into your projector, with the side with the stamped number facing you, and in the sequence you've set up. Draw a diagonal line along their edges from the right side of the first slide to the left side of the last. Felt-tipped pens make good, healthy edge marks, and different colors can be used for different sets. You can thus make up a slide set that is once and for all marked for correct insertion and sequence for any projector. Any missing, out-of-sequence, or upside-down slide will be apparent at a glance.

Presenting Your Slides for Possible Publication

Publishers are always open to new sources of illustrations. It may seem that picture books and magazines feature the work of the same, topnotch professional photographers over and over again, and often they do. But remember that the pros began as amateurs and somehow, one day, managed to sell their first picture. Never hesitate to show your pictures to any potential market. It's a picture editor's delight to discover and underwrite the efforts of a previously unknown or underpublished photographer. An important nature photography book published three years ago relied on professionals as picture sources but included the work of a Manhattan-based weekday tool-and-die maker and weekend photographer. His nature coverage was mostly confined to a nature preserve just across the river from Manhattan, but its variety and scope was as wide as nature itself. He knew his nature and he knew his photography, and his pictures became a featured essay in the book.

In presenting your work, either in person or by mail, exercise the same selectivity as you would in presenting a slide show. Include a variety of subjects – unless only one subject was requested. If you won't be along to identify your slides, label each as to subject. For your own protection, each slide should also be stamped or labeled with your name. Always keep records of who has what. You have every right to expect your material, and all of it, to be returned in good condition within a reasonable length of time.

Slides are best presented in plastic sheets. Every

picture editor has a light box for viewing. Have no fear that your best slides will be overlooked in this sort of presentation. A careful editor invariably checks each slide with a magnifier to see its details. Presenting your slides in a projector tray becomes a problem if the editor does not have the appropriate projector on hand. Call the editor and check on the availability of a projector if you wish to present a show. Otherwise, your slides will be removed from the tray and handled — very dangerous business that — and your sequence disrupted.

Unmounted 8" x 10" or 11" x 14" prints are the best way to present your black-and-white material. More than 50 prints can be contained in one box for simple mailing to and fro, and safe storage while they are at the publishers. As with color, remember to consider variety and pacing in assembling your black-and-whites. If you have sufficient subjects to submit a hundred prints legitimately, the editor will be happy to look at them. But be warned, picture editors are as subject to boredom as anyone else, and you will stand in better stead by whetting their appetites than by burdening them with a repetitious overabundance of prints. And don't be shy in presenting your photographs. Your interest and hard work deserve respect.

About the Author

Patricia Maye first developed an interest in photography as a fine arts student at Brooklyn College. After graduating, she was employed in the *Time-Life Books* picture bureau, and later served as picture editor of *Special Problems*, *Frontiers of Photography*, and *Photographing Nature*, all in the *Life* Library of Photography Series. Ms. Maye now is managing editor of AMPHOTO (American Photographic Book Publishing Company, Inc.) and, as a free lancer, also serves as project director of a forthcoming four-volume photoguide series.

Field Notes

Field Notes

Field Notes

Field Notes

Field Notes

Field Notes